POMPEII

HISTORY, LIFE & AFTERLIFE

POMPEII

HISTORY, LIFE & AFTERLIFE

ROGER LING

TEMPUS

First published 2005
Reprinted 2007

Tempus Publishing Limited
The Mill, Brimscombe Port,
Stroud, Gloucestershire, GL5 2QG
www.tempus-publishing.com

British Library Cataloguing in Publication Data.
A catalogue record for this book is available from the British Library.

ISBN 978 0 7524 1459 1

Typesetting and origination by Tempus Publishing Limited
Printed in Great Britain

CONTENTS

LIST OF ILLUSTRATIONS

TEXT FIGURES

COLOUR PLATES

ACKNOWLEDGEMENTS

This book is the fruit of a long acquaintance with Pompeii, where I have been working, on and off, since 1966. During this time I have benefited from the support and cooperation of successive Superintendents of Antiquities – Alfonso De Franciscis, Fausto Zevi, Maria Giuseppina Cerulli Irelli, Baldassare Conticello and Pier Giovanni Guzzo – and of the site directors who served under them, Stefano De Caro, Antonio Varone and Antonio D'Ambrosio. They must be given pride of place in any list of acknowledgements. At the same time, I have benefited particularly from acting, from 1978 to 1986, as director of the British programme of research in the Insula of the Menander. This project was initiated by the late John Ward-Perkins, and to him I owe an enormous debt, both for giving me the opportunity to carry out a major investigation at Pompeii and for initially stimulating my interest in Roman architecture and town planning.

Specific help with the book has been provided by Henrik Mouritsen, J.P. Wild and my students Mavis Nwokobia and Alessandra Pompili, all of whom have read and commented on parts of the text. Needless to say, none of them is responsible for any errors and eccentricities that remain. In obtaining illustrations I am indebted particularly to Margaret Ward-Perkins for placing John's archive of Pompeian photographs at my disposal and to Derek Trillo, who has both provided original colour images and carried out digitisation of photographs and drawings (funded by a grant from the Faculty of Arts at the University of Manchester). Other sources of illustrations are acknowledged in the captions, but I would like to offer additional thanks to Amanda Claridge, Alison Cooley, Antonella Coralini, Michael Fulford, Salvatore Nappo and Andrew Wallace-Hadrill for searching out material at my request.

But my greatest debt, as always, is to Lesley Ling, who has not only read the whole text and subjected it to her usual searching criticism, but has also been my regular companion in Pompeii, suffering the setbacks and contributing in no small measure to the successes of my various enterprises. Without her, this book could never have been brought to completion.

I

INTRODUCTION

Pompeii is an archaeological site of a unique kind. Buried by the eruption of Mount Vesuvius in AD 79, it was put into a state of arrested development. The city that we now see, with its houses, public buildings and other monuments, streets, city walls, suburban villas and tombs extensively preserved (*1*), is that of the fateful August day its life was cut short. Indeed, Pompeii is often described as having been sealed in a time capsule. This is not strictly true, because, as we shall see, there is evidence of widespread looting and destruction after the disaster. Nonetheless, what remains is still a remarkable snapshot of an ancient city frozen in time. And it is not just the structures that survive. Much of the bric-à-brac of daily life – on most sites reduced to scattered artefacts and pitiful scraps of pottery – remains where it was interred nearly two millennia ago. The paintings on the walls, the mosaics on the floors, the statues in the gardens, the pots and pans of the kitchens, the household silver, the rich woman's jewellery, the messages scratched or painted on walls, even the people themselves, recoverable by a process of injecting plaster into the voids left by their decomposed bodies (*73*) – all potentially await the excavator's spade. Together with the other sites destroyed by the same eruption – notably Herculaneum, Stabiae and Oplontis – Pompeii is an unrivalled mine of information on living conditions in the early years of the Roman Empire.

For details of the eruption we are fortunate to have a first-hand witness. The younger Pliny (C. Plinius Caecilius Secundus), distinguished barrister, bureaucrat and man of letters, has left us two epistles addressed to the historian Tacitus, who had asked for a description to help him in composing an account of the events of 79.[1] Then a youth of 18, Pliny was staying with his uncle, the encyclopaedist Pliny the Elder, who was in command of the Roman fleet stationed at Misenum at the northern end of the Bay of Naples, some 30km (19 miles) from Vesuvius. Towards one o'clock in the afternoon of 24 August they observed a cloud of

1 View of Pompeii and Mount Vesuvius. *Photograph Ward-Perkins collection*

unusual form, shaped like an umbrella pine, rising from the volcano. The elder Pliny, initially fired by a scientist's curiosity to observe the natural phenomenon, but subsequently spurred on by an SOS message from a woman named Rectina who lived at the foot of the mountain, put to sea with a number of ships to mount a rescue mission. It proved impossible to land in the danger area, so Pliny sailed further south to Stabiae, where he came ashore at the villa of a friend named Pomponianus. Pomponianus had already loaded his luggage on boats in readiness to escape, but was prevented from setting sail by a contrary wind. Pliny joined him in waiting for conditions to improve. During the night intense fires were visible raging on the slopes of Vesuvius, and ashes and clinkers fell upon Pomponianus' villa, raising the level in the courtyard to the point that Pliny, who had retired to sleep, was in danger of being trapped in his bedroom. He was roused, and there was a debate as to whether it was better to stay under cover or flee into the open. Since repeated earth tremors were shaking the buildings, threatening imminent collapse, the party opted to make a run for it, strapping cushions on their heads to fend off the rain of clinkers. It was now daybreak – though the sun was blotted out by the clouds of ash – and they made for the beach; but it was still too rough to put to sea. At this point Pliny, who was overweight and suffered from bronchitis, was unable to go further and succumbed to the fumes. The others had to abandon him where he lay. His body was retrieved when it was safe to return the following day.

While this was happening at Stabiae, the younger Pliny remained at Misenum with his mother. But he too was not totally immune from the effects of the eruption. Violent earth tremors during the night forced him out into the open, and at daybreak he observed that the sea had retreated, leaving marine creatures stranded on the beach, and that the sky beyond the bay was occupied by a terrifying black cloud permeated with flashes of lightning. Soon after, this cloud came across the sea and descended on Misenum, forcing Pliny and his mother into flight. They were enveloped in a choking deluge of ash which took away all visibility and caused panic among the crowds of people who followed them. Eventually, however, the fog lifted, revealing the whole countryside covered by a thick layer of ashes similar in appearance to a snowfall. They were able to return to Misenum and await news of the elder Pliny. The earthquakes continued at least another night with sufficient strength to keep them in a state of fear, but there was apparently no repetition of the ash-fall.

Pliny's account can be combined with the stratigraphy of the volcanic deposits over Pompeii and the other buried sites to reconstruct the sequence of events.[2] Vesuvius had evidently not erupted for some centuries prior to 79, and relentless pressure had built up within the volcano's magma chamber. During the morning of 24 August 79, this had blown the plug that sealed it, sending a column of hot ash and pumice thousands of metres into the air, which then spread out to produce the umbrella-pine effect described by Pliny. From here the pumice was carried by the wind southwards and south-eastwards to fall on Pompeii and Stabiae. This stage was not fatal to the inhabitants, and it was possible, as Pliny's account makes clear, for those who so resolved, to get away, protecting their heads against the falling material. Many, however, took refuge in the hope that the crisis would pass. The longer they waited, the greater the danger. The rain of pumice continued until the accumulation reached a thickness of 240cm (almost 8ft), trapping them inside the rooms in which they sheltered, and combining with the effects of the repeated tremors that accompanied the eruption to cause buildings to collapse. But there was a new and more deadly peril. As time went on, the eruptive column became unstable and periodically collapsed, sending out a series of pyroclastic surges – dense clouds of hot gas and ashes which careered down the mountainside at speeds of 100-300km (60-180 miles) per hour. These blasted everything in their path. Early on the morning of the 25th one of them overwhelmed Pompeii. The remaining Pompeians, many of whom had climbed above the earlier falls of pumice in a belated attempt to escape, were instantly asphyxiated. As the fall-out and pyroclastic discharges continued, layers of ash built up until the thickness of the deposits totalled about 5m (over 16ft). The bodies of the victims, together with all of their city apart from the uppermost parts of the buildings still standing, were entombed.

At Herculaneum, lying to the west of the volcano, the end came sooner. The city was covered by at least six pyroclastic surges, burying it to a depth of 20-25m (65-85ft). Those who had not fled immediately – that it was possible to do so is proved by Pliny's report that Rectina had got a note across the bay to Misenum – gathered on the beach to await evacuation by sea, but (as Pliny tells us) it was impossible for boats to land. They never escaped. The remains of more than 250 victims have been found where they were sheltering in vaulted chambers along the sea-front.

The death of Pompeii came at a crucial moment in the history of the western world. The Roman Empire had now expanded to embrace the whole Mediterranean basin and the lands around; it extended south to the Sahara, north to the Danube, and west to the Atlantic; Roman armies were currently tightening the emperor's grip over Britain, with Agricola campaigning in the Pennines and southern Scotland. Within less than 40 years, Roman arms would be carried north to the Carpathian mountains and east to the Persian Gulf. Though these furthermost conquests were later relinquished, the rest remained intact. Never before had such a large area of the earth's surface been brought under a single government for such a long period. Roman civilisation, heavily influenced by that of the Greeks before it, handed down legacies that are fundamental to the modern West, from architectural techniques to legal codes. Its visual arts and literature, filtered through the medium of the Italian Renaissance, formed the basis of artistic style and the classical movement of the seventeenth, eighteenth and nineteenth centuries. Its language contributed much to the Romance languages of present times. Ultimately, its legacy included Christianity, the dominant religion of the western world.

Situated around 200km (125 miles) south-east of Rome, in the wealthy and strongly Hellenised region of Campania, Pompeii was close to the heart of this civilisation in the period of its greatest achievements. The city's history, which can be traced back 600 or 700 years, coincided with the rise of Rome from a local power in central Italy to the mistress of the Mediterranean. Barely a century before the eruption of Vesuvius, the process of transformation was consolidated by the first emperor Augustus, who presided over the dismantling of the old Republican constitution and the development of a structure of professional bureaucrats and standing armies which was to form the basis of imperial government for another 400 years. As a witness to these developments, and as a direct source of information on the material culture of the time, Pompeii acquires especial importance among archaeological sites.

It would, of course, be wrong to regard it as a major centre in its own right. The dominant cities of Campania lay further to the north. On the coast the old Greek colonies of Neapolis (Naples) and Puteoli (Pozzuoli) were flourishing ports with large populations: Puteoli enjoyed particular importance as the focus of Rome's maritime trade with the East, a role that it was to retain until the second century AD, when the construction of a new harbour near Ostia, at the mouth of the River Tiber, wrested away its primacy. Inland, the leading centre was Capua, which stood on the Via Appia, the great arterial road that ran from Rome to Brundisium (Brindisi) at the south-east corner of Italy. Next to these cities Pompeii was comparatively small and insignificant.

Yet it had a certain strategic importance within its immediate region (2). Built on a volcanic spur extruded by an early eruption of Vesuvius, it commanded the mouth of the River Sarno, whose fertile plain separated the volcano from a range of limestone mountains to the south. These mountains, now known as Monti Lattari, formed the spine of the Sorrento peninsula, the land mass on the south side of the Bay of Naples, and they acted as an impenetrable barrier to overland travel in this direction, just as Vesuvius blocked direct communication to the north. The main land-routes to north and south were dictated by these obstacles. Along the shoreline ran a coastal road, leading in one direction via Herculaneum

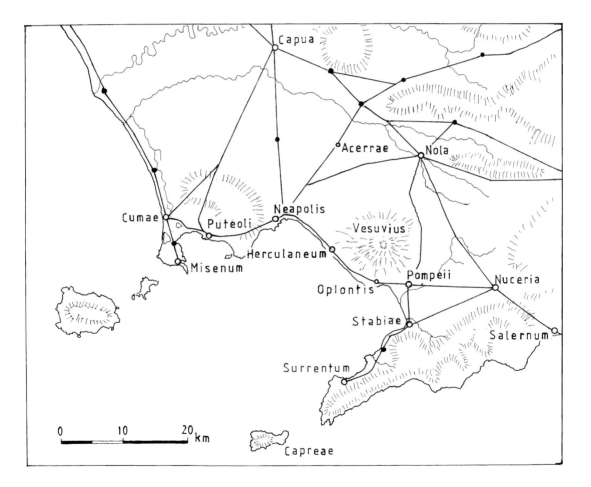

2 Map of southern Campania showing the main centres and lines of communication. *Drawing R.J. Ling*

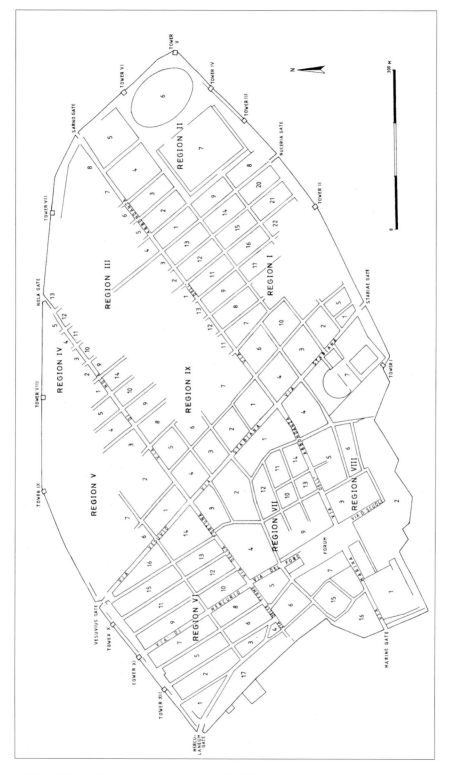

3 Plan of Pompeii in the final phase. *Drawing R.J. Ling*

to Neapolis and Puteoli, in the other via Stabiae to Surrentum (Sorrento). Inland, there was a road that headed eastwards to Nuceria (Nocera), which lay at the entrance of the first convenient pass across the Monti Lattari; here it joined the overland route from Capua to Salernum (Salerno) and the south of Italy. Another road skirted the eastern slopes of Vesuvius to join the same arterial route further north, at Nola. Pompeii's role, given its position, was to provide a maritime outlet for the produce of the Sarno plain and its hinterland (the geographer Strabo says that it was the port not only for Nuceria and Nola but also for Acerrae, further to the north). Though successive volcanic eruptions and changes in sea level have pushed the present coast about 2km (1.25 miles) to the west and diverted the course of the River Sarno further to the south, the city was originally close to the sea and certainly controlled some kind of port at the river mouth. In a pre-industrial era water-borne transport is inevitably cheaper than road-transport, so goods would have been carried from the interior, whether by road or by river, to be shipped at Pompeii. Along with its own production, this commercial activity would have brought the city a degree of economic power and pre-eminence in its corner of Campania.

Figure *3* shows the plan of the city, together with the conventional names given to the gates and principal streets. The area enclosed by the fortifications, roughly elliptical in shape, measures 63.5ha (157 acres). The line of the fortifications was conditioned by the lie of the land. On the south and west, it followed the crest of a steep escarpment, about 30m (100ft) high, which provided a natural defence against attack from these directions; towards the eastern tip the escarpment diminished in height, and along the north side there was only a low saddle, but what was chosen was nonetheless the best line available. Within the walls the levels dropped from north-west to south-east. The slope was especially steep in the central area, where it developed at the south end into a kind of valley between higher terrain to east and west. This naturally dictated the position of the main southern, or Stabiae, Gate and the route of the street that led to it. The street in question, the so-called Via Stabiana (Stabiae Road), acted as the *cardo maximus*, the principal north–south artery, of the city. At its north end (where its name changes to Via Vesuvio) it debouched at the Vesuvius Gate, which gave access to farmland at the foot of the volcano. Running transversally were two main east–west streets (*decumani*). The northern one, formed by Via delle Terme (Baths Street), Via della Fortuna (Fortune Street) and Via di Nola (Nola Road), led to a gate in the north-east sector of the walls, the so-called Nola Gate. The southern one, consisting of Via Marina (Sea Street) and Via dell'Abbondanza (Abundance Street), linked the Marine Gate at the west end with the so-called Sarno Gate at the east.

Within the framework provided by these main through-routes there were grids of intersecting streets. The general principle appears to have been to achieve rectangular or near-rectangular blocks, but there are differences of alignment and of spacing from one area to another, betokening separate phases of development. The most marked anomaly is at the south-west corner where the blocks, or *insulae*, are smallish and less regular than elsewhere. The perimeter of this area is defined by a sequence of streets that form a curving outline; and its interior is bisected by main streets on the east–west and north–south axes – the first corresponding to Via Marina and Via dell'Abbondanza, the second to Via del Foro (Forum Street) and Via delle Scuole (Street of the Schools). The forum, the piazza which constitutes the commercial and administrative hub of the city, sits over the angle formed by the central crossroads. It was recognised by F. Haverfield in 1913 that this quarter represents a primitive nucleus, an 'old town' which preceded the laying out of the 'new town' to the north and east.[3] The blocks which separate the curving perimeter road from the more regular street-systems around it are especially large and irregular, giving the effect of leftover spaces created when it was decided to expand the built-up area and impose a new, more orderly framework.

The remainder of the plan can be divided into three principal parts. The first is represented by a series of large, roughly rhomboidal blocks situated along the east side of Via Stabiana. The second, in the north-west sector, consists of a regular grid of long narrow blocks aligned on a prolongation of Via del Foro, called Via di Mercurio, which produces a slight obliquity in relation to the northern *decumanus* (Via delle Terme and Via della Fortuna) and a strong convergence with the northernmost stretch of the *cardo* (Via Vesuvio). The third, occupying much of the eastern half of the city, is based on a grid of regularly spaced streets crossing Via di Nola and Via dell'Abbondanza at right angles.

Of the city gates those served by the *cardo* and the two *decumani* have been mentioned. Others occurred at the north-west angle and in the southern defences, halfway between the Stabiae Gate and the south-east angle. The north-western one, the Herculaneum Gate, lay at the end of a road which ran at an angle to the remaining streets in this sector, creating a series of irregular triangular *insulae* along its course. The other one, the so-called Nuceria Gate, was at the extremity of one of the north–south streets in the regular grid of the eastern sector. There was no corresponding gate at the north end of this street, which came out close to the Nola Gate; nor was there any further gate in the central part of the northern defences. An old theory that an additional gate may have existed midway between the Vesuvius and Nola Gates, reflecting the line of an early road to Capua, has been disproved by recent excavations.[4]

The city walls, as will be seen in the following chapter, go back at least to the sixth century BC, and examination of their fabric and form reveals a series of remodellings over the course of time. In the final phase they had ceased to have real meaning in military terms; along the west and south-west stretches, enterprising householders had taken advantage of the situation to build over them and create luxurious terraced villas overlooking the bay and the Sarno plain. Along the remaining stretches, however, the walls remained largely intact, a visible statement of civic pride. A series of square towers straddled them at more or less regular intervals. There were three between the Herculaneum and Vesuvius Gates, two between the Vesuvius and Nola Gates, one between the

Nola and Sarno Gates, four between the Sarno and Nuceria Gates, one between the Nuceria and Stabiae Gates, and one more to the west of the Stabiae Gate.

Not all of the city has yet been exposed. Three extensive swathes to the east of Via Stabiana, together amounting to about a third of the intramural area, remain buried 5m (17ft) under the modern ground level (where vine-growing has given way to the less destructive cultivation of flowers and vegetables). However, the isolation of these unexcavated areas, one in the central northern sector, one between Via di Nola and Via dell'Abbondanza, and one in the southern sector, means that we can predict the lines of the missing streets with reasonable confidence; moreover, their position in relation to the known elements of the city fabric suggests that they contained chiefly residential buildings, many of which (especially in the easternmost quarter) would have been comparatively modest in scale.

The public buildings of the city are arranged in clusters, the chief of which are in the south-west sector, focused round the forum and along the west side of Via Stabiana; a further group occupies the south-east corner.

The forum complex (*4*) consists of prominent religious buildings as well as administrative and commercial ones. At the north end, facing down the open piazza, stood the Capitolium, the temple of the three deities Jupiter, Juno and Minerva whose cult held prime position among the religions of the Roman state. Along the west side, immediately to the north of Via Marina, was the temple of the Greek god Apollo. On the east side, facing across the northern half of the piazza, were two temples of Imperial date, the first normally termed the Temple of the Public Lares (guardian deities of the city) but perhaps connected rather with the imperial cult, the second that of the Genius (spirit) of Augustus. Round the south end were grouped various commercial and administrative buildings. Proceeding anti-clockwise, these were the Basilica, an aisled hall employed for judicial proceedings and public meetings, three similarly sized municipal buildings which were used by the city council and executive officers (one may have been the public record office), the Comitium, an open enclosure in which local elections took place, and the Building of Eumachia, normally interpreted as the guild hall of the fullers or as a market building for woollen cloth and luxury goods (for another view, see p. 128). At the north end of the forum, to left and right of the Capitolium, were further market buildings: the Macellum, or fish and meat market, lay to the east, the Forum Olitorium, or vegetable market, to the west.

Other public buildings in close proximity to the forum were the temple of the city's patron deity Venus, which lay behind the Basilica, occupying a terrace that overlooked the harbour and the sea, and the temple of Fortuna Augusta (the protecting fortune of the imperial house), which was situated a block to the north, on the corner of Via del Foro and Via degli Augustali. Immediately opposite this last building, occupying a whole *insula* behind the Capitolium, was a set of public baths, the so-called Baths of the Forum (*24*). Together with the Stabian Baths, which lay in the angle formed by the intersection of Via Stabiana and Via dell'Abbondanza, they catered for one of the most important needs of

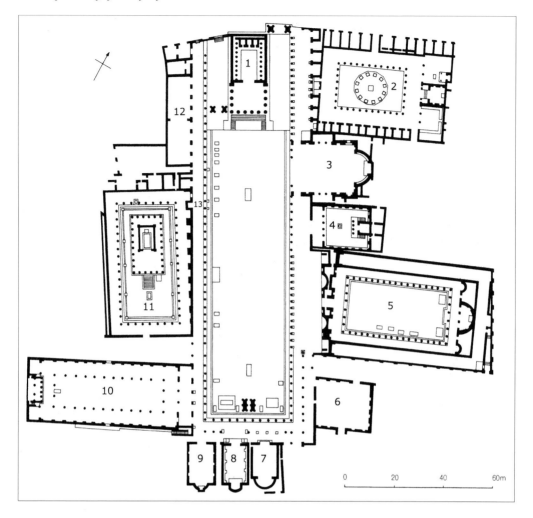

4 Plan of the forum area. 1: Capitolium; 2: Macellum; 3: so-called Temple of the Public Lares (imperial cult building?); 4: temple of the Genius of Augustus; 5: Building of Eumachia; 6: Comitium; 7-9: municipal buildings; 10: Basilica; 11: temple of Apollo; 12: Forum Olitorium. *After J.B. Ward-Perkins and A. Claridge,* Pompeii AD 79 *(1976)*

the dwellers in a Roman city, providing facilities not only for bathing but also for exercise and social contacts. A third set of baths, the Central Baths, situated on the east side of Via Stabiana, immediately next to the Via di Nola crossroads, was still in process of construction at the time of the eruption.

A further group of public buildings was to be found on the west side of the depression through which Via Stabiana descended to the Stabiae Gate (5, 59). On a high platform overlooking the depression, the so-called Triangular Forum contained a temple going back to the sixth century BC, perhaps dedicated jointly to Minerva and Heracles. Further small temples dedicated respectively to the Egyptian deity Isis and (probably) to the Greek god Aesculapius (Asclepius) and a small *gymnasium*, the so-called Samnite Palaestra, were sited on the northern rim of the hillside, and below them, taking advantage of the steep slope for their respective auditoria, were hollowed the large theatre, designed for dramatic and other theatrical performances, and the small or covered theatre, designed for concerts (if not, as recently suggested (see p. 54), for meetings of the Roman colonists who were settled in Pompeii in 80 BC). The group of buildings was completed, behind the stage building of the large theatre, by a colonnaded piazza which may have begun life as a public *gymnasium* but which in 79 was used as barracks for gladiators.

The last major public buildings are those at the eastern end of the city. The amphitheatre, with its vast oval arena hollowed into the subsoil (*6*), nestled in the angle of the city walls, exploiting the rampart inside them to support its seating; here were staged the gladiatorial combats and wild-beast hunts which were a staple form of entertainment in the late Republican and Imperial (Augustan and later) periods. Next to it to the west was the Large Palaestra, a great colonnaded square used for the training of the youth corps established by Augustus in the various Roman cities.

All the other space in Pompeii was given over to private buildings, whether domestic or commercial or both. Generally speaking, the commercial premises – shops and workshops – were concentrated along the streets which were most

5 Aerial view of the theatre quarter. *Photograph Ward-Perkins collection*

6 Interior of the amphitheatre (built *c.* 70 BC). *Photograph R.J. Ling*

frequented, especially the major thoroughfares such as Via Stabiana and Via dell'Abbondanza. Often these premises were small units with a room for trading open to the street and a living room or rooms at the rear (or in a mezzanine or upper storey). But just as often they occupied the front rooms of large houses which extended deep into the *insula*. The juxtaposition of small working establishments and grand residences was as characteristic a feature of Pompeii as it was of the cities of medieval and early-modern Europe. The houses varied in size, the majority measuring no more than about 300sq m (3,230sq ft) in ground area (which of course takes no account of any rooms available on upper floors) but many of them expanding to fill a large part, if not all, of an *insula*.

The names that we give to the streets and gates at Pompeii, and the way in which we designate houses, are entirely modern.[5] There is some evidence for the existence of ancient names for certain streets and for the gates (what we call the Herculaneum Gate, for instance, seems to have been the Porta Salis or Saliniensis, so named after the salt works along the coast to the west of the city), but it is unlikely that the naming was carried out on a comprehensive or systematic basis, and there were certainly no plaques with street names on the walls as there are in most modern cities. Still less were the houses numbered. Ancient cities had no organised postal services, and directions for strangers seeking a particular house or other address were given, as we learn from the New Testament and other literary sources, by citing landmarks and the names of house owners. It is only the present-day visitor who needs more specific indications. These are furnished by a system of postcodes devised in the nineteenth century (cf. *3*). The urban area is divided into nine regions (delimited by the main through-roads), each of which has its constituent *insulae* numbered in a more or less systematic order; and within each *insula* the doorways are numbered in sequence, either clockwise or anti-clockwise. By this means it is possible to express an address in terms of three numbers: thus, for example, VI.9.6 refers to the property entered by the sixth doorway in the ninth *insula* of Region VI (the regions are usually defined in Roman numerals).

In addition to this, most houses have conventional modern names. Some are called after the people who are supposed, rightly or wrongly, to have owned them (the *Praedia* or Domain of Julia Felix, House of the Vettii, House of D. Octavius Quartio) or after the owner's putative profession (House of the Surgeon, House of the Tragic Poet); some take their name from a prominent feature (House of the Small Fountain (*63*), House of the Coloured Capitals), or from a painting or object found in them (House of the Marine Venus, House of the Menander: *colour plates 1, 24*), others from a prominent visitor who came during the excavations (House of Queen Carolina, House of the Prince of Naples) or an event that took place at the time of excavation (House of the Centenary, House of the Silver Wedding).

As for the names given to streets, if they do not simply refer (like the names of the gates) to the neighbouring city or other destination to which they are believed to have led (Nola Road, Stabiae Road), most derive from prominent buildings (Brothel Lane, Street of the Theatres) or from a landmark such as a street-fountain with a carved figure (Cock Lane, Abundance Street: *7, 67*). One or two names are more or less arbitrary (Street of the Augustals, Street of the Schools); one – Vicolo Storto (Crooked Lane) – describes the form of the street itself.

While two thirds of the area within the walls have been exposed, very little is known of the area outside. In the immediate suburbs there have been excavations outside the city gates, revealing the beginnings of the extramural roads and of the cemeteries which (as in all Greek and Roman cities) lined them. In addition to the roads that led to the next cities or into the surrounding countryside, there are remains of a ring road that encircled the walls, enabling traffic to avoid the city if so desired. This, too, became built up with tombs, to judge from the necropolis found outside the Nuceria Gate (*8*). On the west side of the city, where the terrain descended steeply towards the sea, the ring road may have been replaced by the trunk-route along the coast. Outside the Herculaneum Gate, the excavations have been carried some 250m (820ft), revealing that the road towards Herculaneum sent off a fork to the right and a side-turn to the left, the latter presumably linking with the coastal route. Among the tombs in this quarter, which have led to the first part of the Herculaneum road being called Via dei Sepolcri (Street of the Tombs), were three suburban villas – the

7 Relief of a cock on a fountain (south-west corner of *insula* VII.15), which gives its name to the Vico del Gallo (Lane of the Cock). *Photograph L.A. Ling*

Villa of the Mosaic Columns, the Villa of Diomedes and the so-called Villa of Cicero. Further out, in the gap between the main road and the right-hand fork, lies the well-known Villa of the Mysteries. The phenomenon of luxurious villas interspersed with the mausolea of a suburban necropolis can again be paralleled in other ancient cities.

Recent excavations connected with the construction of a monumental entrance to the archaeological site have revealed the road outside the Marine Gate, descending steeply towards the coast. On its north side, nestling under the city walls, is another bath-complex, the so-called Suburban Baths.

Otherwise our knowledge of the surroundings of Pompeii depends on isolated discoveries, many of them the chance results of modern building operations. The city's *territorium* (rural district) presumably extended to meet those of the neighbouring cities (Herculaneum, Nola and Nuceria) roughly halfway; to the south it may have gone no further than the River Sarno, beyond which lay the *territorium* of Stabiae (subsumed within that of Nuceria after the Social War of 91-89 BC). Numerous villas, both grand and modest, have turned up within this area. They include several at Boscoreale, a short distance to the north, two or three at Boscotrecase to the north-west, and (discovered in the 1960s) the vast villa of Oplontis to the west, underlying the modern town of Torre Annunziata. To the south and south-west of the city, intermittent excavations have revealed intensive development on the river-front and coast, including shops and

8 Necropolis outside the Nuceria Gate: monuments SW 5, 7 and 9. *Photograph J.B. Ward-Perkins*

warehouses. The most spectacular discovery, resulting from the construction and subsequent widening of the modern motorway that skirts Pompeii, is a building with elaborate baths and a suite of dining rooms which has been speculatively identified as a luxury hotel.[6]

This survey of Pompei and its *territorium* relates to the situation at the moment of the city's destruction. It is important to note that the study of Pompeii (and of the other sites buried by the eruption of 79) has tended to be different from that of other archaeological sites, in that the excavators have traditionally concentrated their efforts on the final levels. Paradoxically, the very completeness of the city of 79 has militated against the in-depth examination to which other sites are normally subjected. Most Roman remains that have come to us have suffered long periods of decay and disintegration; very often they have been disturbed, if not largely destroyed, by later building, the digging of pits, plough damage or the like. As a result, all that remains are *disjecta membra* – the foundations of walls (or their robbed-out trenches), fragments of wall-paintings, scattered objects out of their original contexts. To interpret such sites, it is axiomatic that modern archaeologists undertake stratigraphical excavations. Because Pompeii has survived largely intact, there is a natural disinclination to probe below the level of 79: to do so extensively and in a systematic manner would involve digging through mosaic or mortar pavements, if not also stripping plaster from walls to observe the underlying structure. Such destructive procedures are clearly

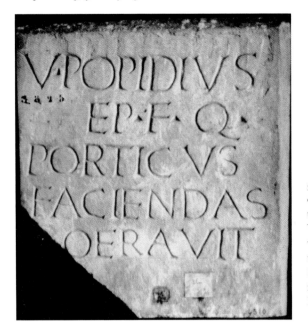

9 Inscribed slab recording the start of work on a colonnade round the forum. The responsible official, V. Popidius, was a quaestor, a post which dates the inscription before the planting of the Roman colony in 80 BC, while the use of Latin places it after the siege of 89. 45.5 x 44cm. Naples Museum 3825. *Photograph Ward-Perkins collection*

unacceptable, if only on the grounds that Pompeii's appeal to the general public – and the way in which it must be packaged for that public – is as a complete city frozen in one moment of time. This means, however, that what is one of the world's best known archaeological sites is in some respects, ironically, one of the least well understood.

The present book will examine life and conditions in the final phase of the city, but it will also seek to reconstruct the earlier periods. There has been an increasing awareness over the last 100 years or so that Pompeii should be studied in terms of its historical development, not just its last years. Analysis of the standing walls, using the evidence of abutments, anomalies in plan, and variations in materials and techniques, coupled with the changing modes of painted wall-decoration, charted first by August Mau as long ago as 1882,[7] enable us to construct a broad chronology. The evidence of inscriptions, both the official ones cut in stone (*9*; cf. *39, 41*) and the unofficial ones scratched or painted on wall-plaster, provide some more specific dates. Since the 1930s there have also been selective excavations beneath the surface of 79, both in houses and in public buildings, often with the specific purpose of addressing chronological issues. A better knowledge of the dating of pottery fabrics contributes to the effectiveness of such *sondages*. It is as a consequence of putting together the fragments of information derived from these various sources that we can now proceed, in the next four chapters, to trace the history of Pompeii phase by phase.

2

POMPEII BEFORE THE ROMANS

The beginnings of Pompeii are hazy. The earliest material from the site goes back well into prehistoric times: to Neolithic times belongs a hand-axe found near the Nola Gate, while the Bronze Age is represented by a deposit of material from the area of the Nuceria Gate. The latter is sufficient to suggest the existence of some form of settlement, but there is no means of telling how extensive this was. Excavations elsewhere in the city and its surroundings have produced little of comparable date, and it is not until the beginning of the sixth century BC that a clearer picture begins to emerge.

This is the time to which we can assign the earliest phase of the city walls.[1] Constructed in a soft local volcanic tuff known as *pappamonte*, remains of these early walls have been exposed at various places beneath the later fortifications, notably at the Herculaneum and Vesuvius Gates and in a stretch close to the Nuceria Gate (where excavations took place in the early 1980s). The dating, which depends on associated pottery of Greek and Etruscan manufacture, has entailed a radical revision of the traditional thinking about the chronology of the city's development. It used to be believed that, while the south-west quarter of the city (the 'old town') went back to the years round 600 BC, Pompeii expanded to its final size only during the fourth century BC – perhaps as the result of an influx of Samnite settlers. It is now clear, however, that the whole area of the final city was already enclosed by walls at least two centuries earlier.

More than this, finds of early house foundations in the same *pappamonte* tuff, together with pottery and other material of sixth-century date (*10*), indicate that the enclosed area was at least partially built up from the start. Particularly important are the results of Anglo-Italian excavations in *insula* I.9, which have revealed what are probably sixth-century structures aligned on the street-grid in

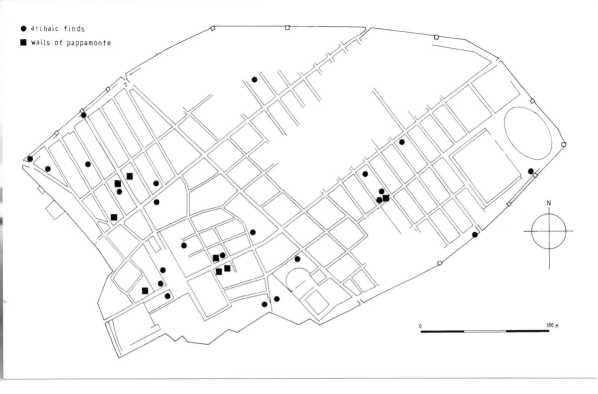

10 Distribution map of archaic finds and walls in *pappamonte*. *Drawing R.J. Ling, adapted from* Papers of the British School at Rome *lxvii (1999), 107, fig. 26*

the eastern part of the city, implying that the full plan, not just that of the south-west quarter, had already been laid out at this date.[2] It is thus clear that attempts to reconcile the traditional chronology with the early dating of the city walls by interpreting the 'old town' as an early development within a much larger walled area, the bulk of which remained undeveloped, must now be discarded. It seems that not only the full circuit of walls but also the final pattern of streets had already been fixed soon after 600 BC.

And yet the street plan clearly betokens a piecemeal development, within which the 'old town' represents the first phase and the eastern quarter the last (*11*). If the whole process was essentially complete by the early sixth century, the first stages must be carried back to an earlier time. How far, we cannot tell, since there are too few excavations into the archaic levels to have supplied the requisite dating evidence. However, the different size, shape and alignment of *insulae*, the central position of the forum, and the presence of the oldest religious sanctuaries (those of Apollo and Minerva/Heracles) – all indicate that the 'old town' enjoyed chronological primacy over the rest. Whether it ever constituted an independent city with its own circuit of defensive walls, cannot be determined without further excavation, but the large size and irregular shape of the *insulae* surrounding the old town – and especially the failure of certain internal streets to cross this framing zone – strongly points to the existence of an obstacle which hindered expansion. This may have been an enclosing ditch and rampart, perhaps reinforced with a palisade, or it may have been a full-blown city wall.

At a later stage the city was expanded to its present extent, and acquired the essentials of an enlarged street-grid. This was based on certain main alignments which determined the positions of the gates and towers along the new circuit of city walls. On the north–south axis the line of Via Stabiana was fixed, as already stated, by the configuration of the land. From west to east, the two main roads Via di Nola and Via dell'Abbondanza ran roughly parallel to the western part of the northern defences and the eastern part of the southern defences, while their spacing was determined by dividing Via Stabiana/Vesuvio into three equal lengths. This resulted in the eastern stretch of Via dell'Abbondanza forming a continuation of the *decumanus* of the old town, albeit with a slight change in alignment. Via di Nola, on the other hand, was projected westwards in a straight line to meet the diagonal road that ran north-west from the old town towards Herculaneum.

The framework of main streets formed the basis round which were constructed the three component parts of the street plan described in Chapter 1. These must represent separate developments, though the intervals between them (or at least that between the first two) need not have been very great. The first stage (*11*, phase 2) is constituted by the series of large rhomboidal *insulae*, two deep, along the east side of Via Stabiana. These are predicated on the alignment of Via di Nola and Via dell'Abbondanza. In Regions I and IX the dimensions of the *insulae* were established by dividing the available space into two, then dividing the two halves to get quarters; the central street in each case was aligned on a tower of the eastern defences, situated respectively midway between the south-east corner of the city and the Sarno Gate (tower VI) and midway between the Sarno and Nola Gates (tower VII). In Region V, the rationale of the division is rather different, in that there is only one east–west street, which lies somewhat to the south of the midpoint; moreover the two *insulae* adjacent to Via Vesuvio are long and narrow rather than equal-sided. It is possible that the arrangements here were dictated by the position of the east–west street dividing Region VI and may thus be later than the layout further south.

The next stage (*11*, phase 3) is the north-west quarter, with the streets oriented on the *cardo* of the old town, which is prolonged as far as the northern defences in the form of Via di Mercurio. There are three pairs of *insulae* to the east of this and three to the west. In the initial phase of the new town, Via di Mercurio apparently passed through the walls into the countryside, but the gateway was subsequently blocked and replaced by a tower which faced down the street much as the towers on the eastern defences faced down east–west streets. More interestingly, the orientation of Via di Mercurio and of the *insulae* that flank it is

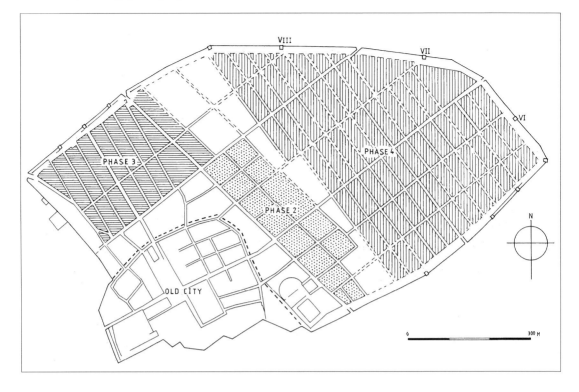

11 Hypothetical plan of the main phases of urban development. Some of the phase 4 *insulae* were later suppressed to make way for the amphitheatre and the Large Palaestra. *Drawing R.J. Ling*

reflected by that of three villas in the north-west suburbs – the Villas of Cicero, of Diomedes and of the Mysteries – all of which display a striking obliquity in relation to Via dei Sepolcri. The same orientation appears also in at least two of the villas at Boscoreale. It has been attractively argued that this orientation was dictated by a system of land allotments based on the alignment of the extramural continuation of Via di Mercurio – a system that may have been created at the same time as, or soon after, the planning of Region VI.[3] It is even possible that the principles adopted in the land division, which may have been similar to those of the 'centuriation' visible round many Roman colonies in northern Italy, determined the layout of the *insulae* within the walls. The width of these *insulae* is a standard 120ft, a unit employed in both Greek and Roman land-surveying, while the length of the more northerly row is roughly 480ft, that is four times the width. The southern row, by contrast, is only about 315ft long, but this disparity is due to the intervention of the newly created *decumanus* formed by Via delle Terme and Via della Fortuna.

The rectangular grid in the eastern part of the city (*11*, phase 4) clearly represents a change of plan in relation to the phase of rhomboidal *insulae* along Via Stabiana. The switch of orientation and the various dislocations where the two systems meet leave little room for doubt on this score. Particularly striking is the suppression of the east–west street which bisected Region I and pointed towards tower VI on the eastern defences. This street terminates abruptly at the south-east corner of *insula* I.10, and from that point eastwards the zone to the south of Via dell'Abbondanza is divided into only three rows of *insulae* rather than four. The principles of measurement guiding the new layout are similar to those in Region VI. The *insulae* are again roughly 120ft wide, while the northern row measures 300ft in length, suggesting a deliberately chosen proportion of 1:2.5. The two remaining rows, which are slightly shorter, each measuring about 280ft, could have been fixed by dividing the residual space in two. Alternatively, as suggested by the Italian archaeologist S.C. Nappo, the lengths of all three rows were based on an equal division but the two southerly rows were reduced by the loss of narrow strips to accommodate the intervening east–west streets and a space inside the fortifications.[4] In either case, it is noteworthy that the street dividing the middle and southernmost rows lines up with the street separating the two southernmost *insulae* on the east side of Via Stabiana: since the division between these two *insulae* is surprisingly unequal, it may have been created by prolonging the corresponding street of the new quarter.

Details of the arrangements in the two northern sectors of the new quarter (Regions III and IV) are uncertain because of the incompleteness of the excavation, but the *insulae* had the same width of 120ft, and there was probably in each case a single transversal division, that of Region III continuing the line of the central east–west street of Region IX, and that of Region IV prolonging that of the east–west street within Region V.

As in Region VI, there may have been a correlation between the layout of this new quarter and a system of land allotments outside the walls. Excavations in the area of the necropolis outside the Nuceria Gate have revealed traces of fields on the same alignment as the intramural grid.[5]

Much discussion has focused on the city's ethnic origins. Was it founded by an indigenous people or was it a colony planted by Greeks or other intruders? The etymology of the name 'Pompeii' is uncertain, so cannot be used to resolve the issue. The various derivations that have been touted include words both in the language of the Oscans, native to the region, and in Greek. A possible link with the Oscan word *púmpe*, meaning 'five', has led to a theory that the city originated in the union of five villages or that there was some form of fivefold division of the citizen body. If this were tenable, it would strengthen the case for a native foundation. Alternatively the name may be connected with the Greek word *pompe* in the sense of 'procession', referring to some important religious celebration (an alternative idea – that *pompe*, literally 'sending', could have alluded to the city's role, specifically described by the geographer Strabo, in dispatching the produce of the hinterland – is less plausible).[6]

Against a Greek foundation is the lack of Greek inscriptions from the early period. A further argument arises from the irregularity of the street plan. Most

Greek colonies in southern Italy and Sicily were laid out with a rigid grid of parallel streets and long rectangular blocks. Such was certainly the case with Herculaneum and Naples. The only parts of Pompeii's plan to conform to this principle, however, are the north-western and eastern sectors, which (as we have seen) belong to secondary phases in the city's evolution. The plan of the old town, though displaying a tendency to regularity, lacks the rigid formality of true Greek cities, and the blocks are squarish rather than elongated rectangles. There may have been some influence from neighbouring Greek cities, but the layout does not suggest an original Greek foundation.

We shall probably never know the right answer, but the balance of probability tilts in favour of native origins. At the same time, evidence is increasing for strong Etruscan influence in the early years. The Etruscans established a widespread political and military hegemony in northern and central Italy during the seventh and sixth centuries BC, a hegemony that extended as far south as Campania and was not finally broken until the Greek victories at Cumae in 524 and 474. That Pompeii used much *bucchero* pottery of Etruscan manufacture is attested by numerous finds in the archaic levels. This does not prove that the city was under Etruscan control, given that the pottery could have been imported. More cogent is the presence on the pottery of graffiti in the Etruscan language, some of which give Etruscan name forms: while few in number, these are sufficiently numerous to imply an actual Etruscan presence.[7] Whether or not Pompeii was originally established by a native people, it seems likely that the Etruscans, seeing the potential of the site for commanding the entrance of the Sarno valley and the coastal route from Naples and Herculaneum to the Sorrento peninsula, soon took control of it.

This interpretation fits neatly with the tradition recorded by Strabo, who, writing at the end of the first century BC, states that the city was 'once held by the Oscans, then by the Tyrrheni and the Pelasgi, and after that by the Samnites'.[8] He is clearly referring to three successive phases, of which the first indicates an early period of native domination and the second a period in which Etruscans (Tyrrhenians) played a dominant role. What is meant by the Pelasgi is less certain. One interpretation, seeing the Pelasgians as mythical Greek colonists from whom the Etruscans claimed descent, takes 'Tyrrheni and Pelasgi' as being merely a periphrasis for the early Etruscans; another sees the Pelasgians as a separate native people with which the Etruscan overlords of Pompeii intermixed. We have no means of deciding which.

The sixth-century city was already, therefore, laid out along the lines that obtained at the time of its destruction in AD 79. Of the houses of this early stage we know too little to make any meaningful assessment, but it is a reasonable conjecture that the most intensive development was in the older south-west quarter. Here there were certainly at least two religious sanctuaries. That of Apollo occupied the position of the later temple, to the west of the forum; excavations have yielded sixth-century architectural terracottas as well as Corinthian pottery datable between about 575 and 550 and Attic pottery of the following half-century.[9] The so-called Doric Temple, thought to have been dedicated to Minerva, if not also Heracles, can be dated to the second half of the century on the basis of the style of its columns, in the archaic form of the Greek Doric order, and of its terracotta revetments. Further sanctuaries are also known from outside the city, notably one in the Bottaro district, in the area of the presumed river-port, from which comes a votive deposit running from the sixth century BC down to the first.[10]

The situation within the city remains difficult to decipher during the fifth, fourth and third centuries. Although the street system appears to have been essentially complete, the northern and eastern parts of the city were probably not fully built up. Excavations in the House of the Etruscan Column (VI.5.17) and in VII.4 have produced evidence that these areas of the city remained at least partially wooded.[11] Studies of palaeobotanical and palaeozoological material from the excavations in I.9.11 and 12 paint a similar picture of relatively sparse occupation before the Roman period. The presence of wood or yellow-necked mice, in particular, points to an environment that was somewhat overgrown, if not actually wooded.[12]

But this period witnessed important political developments. In the fifth century Etruscan control of the region was weakened, and during the fourth century the spread of the Samnites from the mountains of central Italy brought a new element into the racial mix. Pompeii, as Strabo tells us, came under Samnite control. At the same time, the expansion of Rome, which prosecuted a series of wars against the Samnites during the late fourth and third centuries, cast a tall shadow over the region. By the mid-third century Rome was mistress of most of Italy and, while Pompeii and other cities were nominally free allies of the superpower, their capacity for independent action was severely circumscribed.

This changing political and military situation was reflected by changes in the architecture of Pompeii's defensive walls and gates. The structural sequence was charted in 1930 by A. Maiuri, who sought to link it with historical developments and with a hypothetical chronology of house-types and building techniques.[13] Unfortunately the dating evidence for the individual phases, and therefore the precise occasion for each rebuilding, are far from secure. The first major change was when the sixth-century *pappamonte* walls were replaced by a double curtain constructed in the so-called Sarno stone, a calcareous sedimentary rock quarried in the Sarno valley. This happened perhaps at the end of the sixth or the beginning of the fifth century BC, in which case it may represent a strengthening of the city defences in connection with the wars between the Etruscans and the Greeks. Somewhat later, perhaps in the early third century, a new defensive system with a single wall of Sarno stone backed by a wide rampart took the place of the double curtain (*12*). Once again it is impossible to know what prompted the decision to rebuild, but it probably had something to do with the conflicts between the Samnites and the Romans.

12 City walls in Sarno stone, near the Nola Gate. Early third century BC? *Photograph Ward-Perkins collection*

It is doubtful whether any of the standing structures within the city – apart from the Doric Temple – goes back beyond the latter years of the third century. Such hints as we have of building activity in the fifth, fourth and early third centuries are derived from chance survivals (such as a late fourth- or third-century metope (*13*) and architectural terracottas which attest a refurbishment of the Doric temple) or from in-depth excavations such as those in VI.5 and I.9. One structure of interest is a supposed *hestiatorion*, a Greek-style public dining establishment, located by excavations beneath the House of the Clay Moulds (VII.4.62); this is dated on ceramic evidence to the fourth or third centuries BC.[14] Also probably ascribable to this period are the early phases of the Stabian Baths, identified by H. Eschebach from his investigations within the second-century complex.[15]

The late third and early second centuries mark a new stage in the history of Pompeii. It is at this time that the earliest of the houses still standing in 79 seem to have been put up. There is little doubt that they belong to a concerted programme in which existing houses were swept aside to make space for new ones and areas of the city which had been sparsely populated were fully built up. Many of the new properties, especially in Regions I and II, seem to have conformed to a standard size (8.5-10m wide x either 17-20 or 32-35m long) and

13 Sculptured metope from the Doric Temple: Athena, Hephaestus and Ixion. 71cm x 1.47m. Late fourth or third century BC. *Photograph German Archaeological Institute Rome 61.2870*

give the appearance of representing a formal division of available land into equal plots. A recent and persuasive theory sees them as the result of public measures to house an influx of refugees settling in Pompeii during Rome's war with Hannibal, in which cities such as Capua and Nuceria were sacked by the rival armies.[16]

Many of the new houses were built in continuous series similar to modern 'terraced houses', with a standard layout now named the 'Hoffmann type' after the modern investigator who first drew attention to it.[17] Using as examples a row of houses in *insula* I.11, Hoffmann defined a model in which a front and back range, each consisting (usually but not invariably) of two rooms flanking a central passage, framed a cross-hall occupying the full width of the plot; behind the back range was a shallow garden (*14*). He proposed that both the front and back ranges carried an upper floor, whereas the central hall rose the full height of the building; the whole was spanned by a double-pitched roof sloping down to front and rear, with a transversal ridge beam supported by a timber truss constructed over the central space. More recently this reconstruction has been modified, in the light of further information acquired in the *insulae* along Via di Nocera (I.13-15 and 20-21, and II.8 and 9), by S.C. Nappo.[18] He argues that many of the plots were twice as long as Hoffmann believed, extending the full

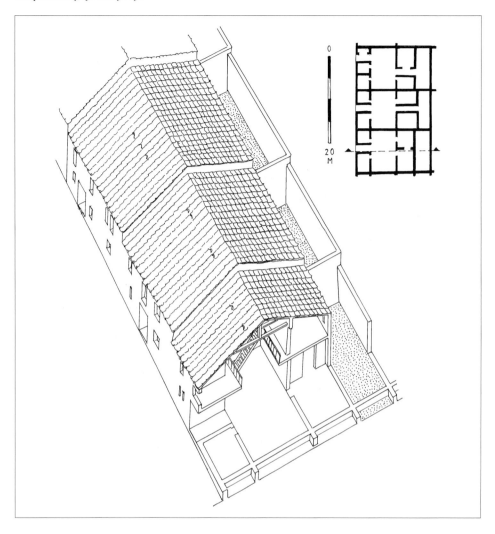

14 Plan and isometric reconstruction of so-called Hoffmann houses (I.11.13-15). *Drawing L.A. Ling, after A. Hoffmann, in F. Zevi (ed.),* Pompei 79 *(1979)*

width of the *insulae* rather than being divided into two separate plots set back to back; and, more controversially, working from detailed observation of clues in the standing masonry, he claims that the houses – at least in their original state – had only one storey and that the central 'hall' was actually an open court. The front and rear rooms were simply covered by single-pitch roofs resting on the walls. This new interpretation is not without its problems: the buildings seem surprisingly prodigal in their use of space, and the two front rooms are oddly isolated from the rest of the covered accommodation. But it would be dangerous to resist the archaeological evidence, and the Nappo formula has the virtue of offering houses which would have been comparatively easy to construct.

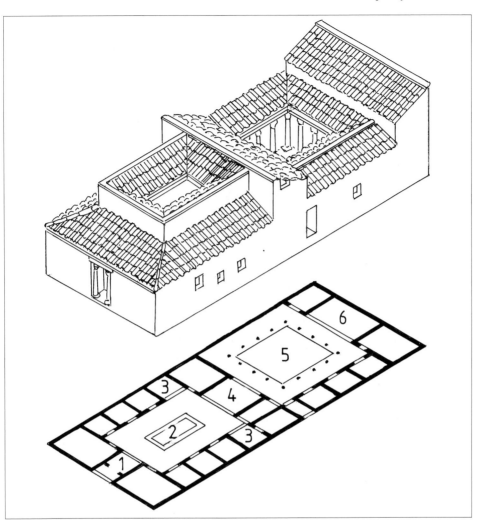

15 Ideal plan and isometric reconstruction of an *atrium* house. 1: *fauces*; 2: *atrium*; 3: *alae*; 4: *tablinum*; 5: peristyle; 6: *exedra*. The room names are derived from Vitruvius. *Drawing L.A. Ling, adapted from E. La Rocca and M. and A De Vos,* Guida archeologica di Pompei *(1976)*

   Alongside these 'Hoffmann houses', the wave of building in the late third and early second centuries included examples of the so-called *atrium* house. In terms of its organisation of space, the *atrium* house is not radically different from the Hoffmann one. Its nucleus is again a rectangular distribution space which is approached from the street by a passage and which gives access to the main living and reception rooms. But there are a number of distinctive features. In the ideal layout (15), the distribution space (the *atrium*) is roofed apart from a central opening, the *compluvium*, designed to admit light and to catch rainwater; there are rooms not only at front and back but also at the sides, and the arrangement of rooms tends to be symmetrical, with an axial entrance passage (the *fauces*), a central reception room at the rear (the *tablinum*), and a pair of open-fronted rooms facing each other at the sides (the *alae*, or wings). In practice, the variations on the theme are innumerable. Sometimes, if space is in short supply, one or both of the side-ranges are suppressed; the *alae* are now at the middle, now at the back, of the side-range; the *tablinum* may be displaced to one side, or even omitted; and so forth. Even the *compluvium* is not an indispensible element and, where present, it is sometimes accommodated within a roof arrangement that precludes the collection of rainwater.

The origins of the *atrium* house are shrouded in uncertainty. A recent study by Andrew Wallace-Hadrill has suggested that the *atrium* began as an open court rather similar to those of the Hoffmann houses; only simple verandahs or porticoes occasionally protected the entrances of certain rooms or provided sheltered walkways for residents passing from one side of the *atrium* to another.[19] Some sustenance to this theory is afforded by the results of excavations which have revealed that in certain *atrium* houses the *impluvium*, the shallow catchwater basin in the floor which is the normal concomitant of the *compluvium* in the roof, was apparently secondary: there seems to have been an earlier floor-surface which lacked this central feature. Thus, if Wallace-Hadrill is right, the distinction that has been drawn between the first *atria* and the courtyards of Hoffmann houses is largely artificial: functionally and architecturally they were the same thing. Indeed, the court in some Hoffmann houses (e.g. I.11.14 and II.9.2) was subsequently turned into a conventional *atrium* by the insertion of an *impluvium*.

But the jury has to remain out. Impluviate *atria* certainly appeared in other parts of Italy, including Rome, long before the late third century BC; and it is possible to argue that the supposed early surfaces without *impluvia*, many of which were of beaten earth, did not represent a separate phase but were merely make-up layers beneath the level of the first pavement. In other cases the insertion of a secondary *impluvium* may have removed all evidence of a pre-existing one. All that we can say for certain is that by 200 BC the standard *atrium* was an established feature of Pompeian domestic architecture.

One important factor in the emergence of the *atrium* must have been the house's need of an adequate, year-round water-supply. In the early period Pompeii had relied on wells, several of which have been discovered underlying and pre-dating the houses of the late third and early second centuries. But the low level of the water table under the hill on which the city stood meant that these had to be dug to a tremendous depth, in some cases as much as 39m (128ft). Moreover, the springs tapped by the wells yielded water that contained sulphur and was not especially pleasant to drink. By collecting and storing rainwater, which was channelled from the *impluvium* into an underground cistern, householders were able to provide themselves with water that was both easier of access and more palatable to the taste. It was, of course, perfectly feasible to collect rainwater without an *impluvium*; indeed there are countless courtyards and gardens at

Pompeii where water was gathered into similar underground cisterns by means of simple gutters and drains. But a sunken basin such as the *impluvium*, situated beneath a central opening towards which all roofs converge, offers a particularly efficient method of capturing the torrential downpours characteristic of the Vesuvius region while sparing the surrounding pavement from the effects of backwash.

The structural techniques of the houses built at the turn of the third and second centuries are based on the use of locally available materials, notably Sarno stone. This was employed chiefly in a technique variously known as *opus africanum* (African work), *opera a telaio* (loom-work), or 'post and panel work', in which large blocks of roughly rectangular shape were set horizontally or vertically to form a framework enclosing panels of small rubble in the same material (*16*);[20] in the early stages, at least, no mortar was employed, the structure being held together by the system of weights and balances embodied in the main blocks; only the rubble infill was given additional stability by a packing of stiff clay. Sometimes the rubble was in a different material, a hard grey-black lava, which contrasted with the Sarno framework to produce a distinctive two-tone, black and white, wall. In the larger houses, however, the façades often replaced post and

16 Opera a telaio: façade of I.10.16. Large blocks of Sarno stone, set horizontally and vertically, form a framework which was infilled with rubble in the same material. Late third or early second century BC. *Photograph R.J. Ling (Pompeii Research Committee 1981-1/18A)*

panel work with an altogether more monumental treatment, namely large blocks of Sarno stone laid in regular courses of ashlar masonry. This technique, found also in the city walls (*12*) and clearly inspired by public architecture, is an early indicator of the aspirations of wealthy Pompeians to the trappings of grandeur.

During the course of the second century domestic architecture was characterised – at least in the houses of the city elite – by an increasing pretentiousness. As in other parts of Italy, the expansion of Roman power into the eastern Mediterranean brought opportunities for entrepreneurs to make fortunes and at the same time introduced a fashion for Hellenistic luxury. One of the most striking testimonies to this trend is the appearance of columnar architecture in the home. Some of the houses of the beginning of the second century had had a single portico behind the *tablinum*, no doubt facing on to an open space or garden, but by the middle of the century it was becoming increasingly common for this portico to expand into a four-sided cloister, or 'peristyle', embracing the garden (*15*). Round the peristyle opened various rooms and open-fronted recesses, or *exedrae*, where the householder could sit and read or enjoy the view, remote from the noise of the street. The very name 'peristyle' (roughly translatable as 'enclosed by columns'), being derived from Greek, betrays a Hellenistic pedigree. The most likely inspiration for the architectural form is the *gymnasium*, a colonnaded area for the physical and intellectual education of the gilded youth in Hellenistic cities. The fact that this was a public building type incorporated into a private house is eloquent of the aspirations of the patrons for whom peristyles were built; but more specifically the association of the *gymnasium* with philosophy and learned discourse made a clear statement about the householder's cultural credentials.

In social terms the importance of the addition of the peristyle was that it changed the functioning of spaces within the house.[21] Previously the *atrium* had been the hub of all activity, the place where the householder both conducted business and entertained friends. The effect of adding a new, more secluded, area at the rear was to create a stronger differentiation between the house's public and private life. Official callers were still received within the *atrium* complex, but only specially invited friends and associates came through to the peristyle and its surrounding rooms. This is not to exaggerate the private nature of the peristyle: the Pompeian house, especially where the owner was a citizen holding or aspiring to public office, was always permeable in a way that modern houses are not. But the creation of a second nucleus enabled a grading of accessibility: to be received in the peristyle quarter was a privilege not granted to all. The shift of prestige from the *atrium* to the peristyle is emphasised by the fact that the house's largest and most richly decorated rooms now tended to be those round the new nucleus, while the rooms at the back of the *atrium* were turned round to face the garden. The *tablinum*, which had originally been closed at the rear except, possibly, for a window (access to the early garden had been via a corridor or corridors at the sides), was increasingly thrown open to become a Janus-like room accessible from either the *atrium* or the peristyle, or simply a passage between the two.

The use of columns was not confined to the peristyle. One or two *atria* had columns at the corners of the *impluvium*, supporting the roof structure above and enhancing the grandeur of the space. Pilasters of Greek type, crowned by Corinthian or 'sofa' capitals, or sometimes by capitals with heads or busts emerging from foliage, were used to frame street doorways. In all cases the objective was clearly to distinguish the houses of the elite from the more modest dwellings around them.

To produce the fine carved detail of columns and pilasters, as well as the mouldings of *impluvium* rims, a new material came into play: the grey or brown tuff from the region of Nuceria. Formed from coagulated volcanic dust, this material was soft and easy to work when first exposed in the quarry but hardened on contact with the air, and it had a much closer and smoother texture than either Sarno stone or black lava. It was thus better suited to the production of sharp angles, subtle profiles and decorative elements. Alongside its use for columns and *impluvia*, it also came to be employed for ashlar façades, sometimes in blocks with drafted or offset margins imitating those of monumental Greek architecture.

For basic construction, especially of internal walls, the coarser materials remained the norm (as they did throughout the history of Pompeii). But the second century saw a major technical development: the introduction of mortar. This material, probably discovered towards the end of the third century BC as the outcome of experiments with a *pisé* (rammed clay) technique of a type familiar in North Africa, was made by mixing lime, water and a gritty substance such as sand. Combined with a rubble aggregate, it became the basis of the concrete construction which was to revolutionise ancient architecture during the next three centuries: strongly cohesive and durable, it was particularly effective for the building of vaults and domes, in which it gave builders the means of spanning interior spaces much greater than was possible with traditional stone or timber roof structures. At Pompeii its chief role was in the so-called *opus incertum*, a walling technique of mortared rubble with a more or less neat facing of roughly fist-sized pieces of stone (*17*). This was a relatively simple form of construction, since it dispensed with heavy blocks, careful shaping, and the calculation of weights and counterweights; once properly set, the mortar bonded the wall into a homogeneous mass. It was also enormously economical, because it absorbed the waste from stone-cutting, and the debris of any demolition could be easily recycled in subsequent periods. As a result, *opus incertum* remained the favourite structural technique until the city's end. The types of stone used in the facing varied from wall to wall, and it is difficult to discern any chronological pattern, save that the standard materials were always Sarno stone and the local volcanic materials black lava and (to a lesser extent) the red or purple vesicular lava known in Italian as *cruma* (English 'lava crust' or 'scoria'), but these were supplemented from the mid-first century BC by the friable yellow tuff from the Campi Phlegraei, north of Naples. During the first century AD, and especially

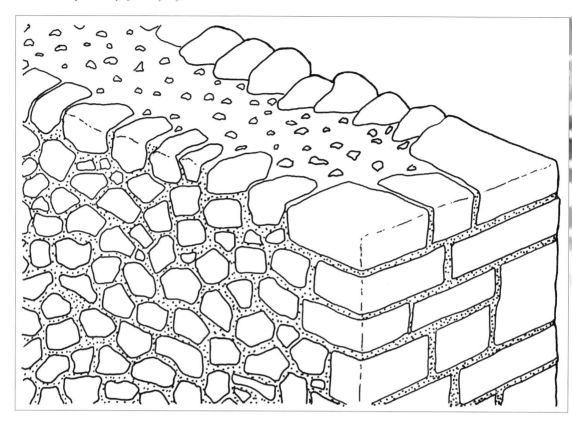

17 Diagram of construction in *opus incertum. Drawing after H. and R. Leacroft,* The Buildings of Ancient Rome *(1969), fig. 10*

in the emergency repairs that followed the earthquake of AD 62, there was an increasing use of heterogeneous materials, including fragments of tiles and odd pieces of white limestone and marble. In the best construction, materials were graded according to their properties. A frequent mode, especially where a wall was exposed to weathering, involved the use of the stronger, more damp-resistant lava to face the lower part, to a level of approximately 1m (3ft), and the lighter, more porous Sarno stone above. In many if not most cases, however, even on the exterior of buildings, the fabric of the wall would be hidden by a layer of plaster, whether to hide what was regarded as an unfinished or unsightly surface, or to provide additional protection against the elements.

Alongside the development of pretentious houses, the second century saw the construction of some of the public buildings which were to shape the urban landscape throughout the rest of the city's existence. Many were Greek in style and function. At the centre of the city, for example, the Stabian Baths were rebuilt in monumental form, supplanting the earlier, simpler establishment, and their combination of a colonnaded exercise ground (the *palaestra*) with sequences of cold, warm and hot rooms (one set for men and one for women) introduced what was almost certainly a Hellenistic fashion, derived from the *gymnasia* of the East; the main difference from the *gymnasium* was that the Pompeian version played down the role of physical training, reducing the proportion of space occupied by the *palaestra*, and put the emphasis on bathing. The heating of the baths probably exploited the latest technology, channeling hot air under the floors in a system whose Greek name 'hypocaust' ('heated underneath') strongly suggests that it too was imported from the East.

In the south of the city was built the first theatre. A specifically Greek institution and building type, long established in the cities of southern Italy and Sicily but excluded from Rome by the prejudices of the ruling aristocracy, the theatre offers a clear indication of the extent to which Hellenistic culture now permeated the city. The initial building is likely to have copied the standard Greek format, with a horseshoe-shaped auditorium enclosing a circular 'dance floor', or *orchestra*, with an independent stage-building (*scaena*) behind it. The performance would have been divided, Greek-style, between the *orchestra* and a high, shallow stage (*proscenium*) attached to the front of the stage-building.

Behind the theatre was a large colonnaded piazza, or quadriportico, surrounded by a series of rooms and open-fronted *exedrae* (5, 59). Normally regarded as a place where theatre-goers congregated before, between and after performances, it has recently been reinterpreted by the German writer Paul Zanker, resuscitating an older theory of August Mau and Matteo Della Corte, as a true Hellenistic *gymnasium*.[22] The architectural form, closely paralleled in several eastern cities, certainly speaks in favour of this interpretation, and a slight misalignment with the stage-building implies that the quadriportico and the theatre were not originally conceived as part of a single project, a circumstance that weakens the argument for a functional relationship. If the quadriportico began life as a *gymnasium* (in the city's last phase it had been converted into accommodation for gladiators), this would represent a further sign of the extent to which Greek culture affected Pompeii.

Overlooking the theatre and the putative *gymnasium*, the precinct of the old Doric temple was now modernised, being framed by colonnades and prefaced by a monumental gateway from the street to the north.[23] This precinct, given triangular shape by the dictates of topography, was planned in the manner of many Hellenistic temple-sites of the Aegean area, not to mention the contemporary terraced sanctuaries of central Italian cities such as Praeneste (Palestrina) and Tibur (Tivoli), to be open on one side, offering a panorama of the Sarno valley and the mountains beyond it. As elsewhere in Italy, the temple seems to have had a close relationship with the neighbouring theatre, whose auditorium was entered by doorways in the precinct wall. But whether this meant that the deity or deities exercised a protective role in relation to the theatrical performances, or even that the theatre was sometimes used for religious ceremonies or sacred plays, it is impossible to know.

Other public buildings which apparently go back to the second century BC are the so-called Samnite Palaestra, to the north of the theatre, and the precursor of the temple of Aesculapius, to the north-east. The original form of the temple is uncertain because of later rebuilding, though a monumental altar of Nuceria tuff in the forecourt probably belongs to the second-century phase, but the Samnite Palaestra survived unaltered apart from the loss of some space at the east end. Dedicated according to an inscription by a magistrate of the Samnite period,[24] it consisted of a colonnaded court with a few rooms on one side and can be identified as a small *gymnasium* designed for an elite club or for boys too young to use the adult version.

Not only the theatre quarter but also the forum area (*4*) saw monumental rebuilding in this period. While the east side, at least, remained lined with small shops and workshops, new public edifices sprang up to the north and south. At the north was erected the axial temple which dominated the square. What precise form this took, and whether it was already dedicated to Jupiter, as it was later, we cannot say. Next to it, on the other side of Via del Foro, there was a predecessor of the later Macellum. At the south end may have stood administrative buildings, antecedents of the trio in existence in AD 79. Most spectacular of the forum buildings of this phase, however, was the Basilica, constructed at the south-west corner. One of the earliest surviving examples of a building type which was destined to be influential both in Roman civic architecture and in the development of Christian churches, this took the form of a large rectangular hall divided internally by massive columns into a nave and a pair of aisles which turned across at the ends (*colour plate 2*). A date within the second half of the second century is assured by the form of the architectural detail and by the presence of tile-stamps and graffiti in the Oscan language.

To the north of the Basilica the temple of Apollo was rebuilt and, somewhat later, received a new pavement of coloured stone, donated by a magistrate of the Samnite period.[25] It is possible that the god's sanctuary now acquired its grand symmetrical layout with a colonnaded precinct on a slightly divergent alignment from that of the forum, but this remains uncertain: there is evidence that points to radical replanning at a later stage (p. 69).

All these buildings, with their use of a Greek architectural vocabulary, are eloquent of the prevalence of Hellenistic culture in the city's Samnite phase. Even more eloquent is the wave of Greek-inspired decorations which characterise the grand houses of the second half of the second century and the early years of the first.

Some of these houses attained a scale and degree of luxury that was virtually unprecedented among known dwellings of the Hellenistic world. None more so than the palatial House of the Faun, which occupied a whole city-block some 2,950sq m (31,750sq ft) in area (*18*). This, in its final form, contained not one but two peristyles, the first with 28 columns, the second with 44. It also had two *atria* side by side, a phenomenon found in some other houses of the period, such as

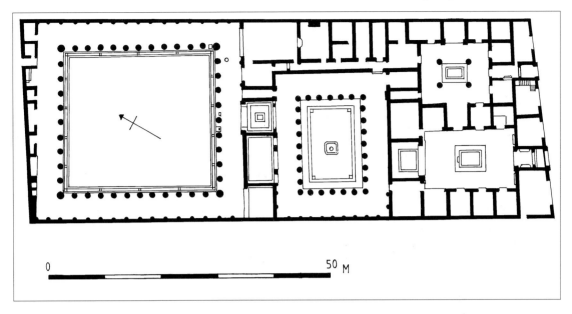

18 Plan of the House of the Faun (VI.12.2). *Drawing L.A. Ling*

the House of M. Obellius Firmus and that of the Labyrinth. One assumes that these *atria* were differentiated in their roles: the larger one would have served primarily for the conduct of public business and the reception of visitors on whom the patron wished to make a strong impression; the other would have been used for more intimate functions and the everyday activities of domestic life.

In the House of the Faun the higher status of the larger (western) *atrium* was confirmed by the greater richness of the wall- and floor-decorations in the rooms around it. The wall-decorations were largely non-representational, with the plaster worked into shallow relief to imitate blocks of drafted masonry, which were then painted in varied colours simulating different types of exotic stone. This mode of decoration, now known as the 'First Pompeian Style', was based on a formula adopted from the Hellenistic cities of the East, but, whereas the eastern examples had remained relatively faithful to the syntax of constructed masonry, the Pompeian versions (along with those of Herculaneum and other Italian sites) became more fanciful both in the arrangement and proportions of the scheme and in the distribution of colours (*colour plate 3*).[26] Any figural elements were normally confined, as in the East, to a narrow zone set more or less at eye level (in one room of the House of the Faun there was a frieze of vine tendrils accompanied by birds, insects and flowers), but occasionally further figures emerged from the play of veins in fictive blocks of marble or alabaster.

While the wall-decorations abjured elaborate pictorial elements, there was no such restraint in the pavements. Here finely worked scenes made of minute tesserae (as little as 2mm square) in stones of carefully graded colours occupied the centre of the floor, where they could be viewed from the doorway or from couches round the walls. An amorous encounter between a satyr and a maenad, the male and female followers of the wine god Dionysus, adorns a bedroom; a display of different species of marine fauna such as might have been served at the table embellishes a dining room. Another room shows a winged child (a Dionysiac spirit?) seated on a tiger, still another a cat mauling a hen. In rooms of passage – the *fauces, atrium* and *tablinum* – there were larger panels of pieces of stone cut to geometric shapes, including the favourite Hellenistic motif of rhombs in three colours so arranged as to create an optical illusion of perspectival cubes. But eclipsing all other pavements was the fabulous Alexander mosaic, a composition illustrating a crucial moment of the battle of Gaugamela (331 BC) in which Alexander the Great defeated the Persian army under Darius (*colour plate 4*). This huge scene, 2.70m high x 5.12m long (approximately 9 x 17ft), contains dozens of figures in a mêlée of violent movement which exploited all the tricks of *trompe l'oeil* including shading, highlights and bold foreshortening: it was evidently a translation into stone of a famous historical painting of the late fourth century BC. Its position within a columnar *exedra* between the first and second peristyles, directly on the axial sightline running through the *fauces, atrium* and *tablinum*, was clearly chosen to emphasise its importance. How far the *exedra* was a functioning room is uncertain. It would have made no sense to place furniture on the mosaic, and one suspects that the space served merely as a showplace for the owner's prize work of art.

Producing such mosaic pictures involved a high measure of skill, and to acquire them must have been expensive. Unlike the wall-paintings, however, they did not have to be executed *in situ*. The smaller panels, often set on tiles or in stone trays, could be shop-bought pieces: indeed the subjects of those in the House of the Faun can be paralleled in other houses at Pompeii, as well as in other Italian cities, suggesting that there were certain popular compositions which the mosaic ateliers reproduced time and again. Some panels may have been imports from the East. Two exquisite pieces depicting theatrical scenes, found in the so-called Villa of Cicero, are signed by an artist from Samos, an island in the eastern Aegean (*19*). Once arrived in Pompeii, they would have been fitted as 'inserts' (*emblemata*) within simply patterned, or unpatterned, surrounds carried out on the spot by local craftsmen. It is possible that even the Alexander mosaic was imported. Mistakes in the details, and particularly the misplacement of certain elements, are most easily explained as the result of reassembling a pavement which had been divided into small pieces for ease of transport.[27]

In addition to mosaic pictures and First Style wall-decorations, we must imagine that the decorative ensembles of houses like that of the Faun would have been completed by wooden furniture, brightly coloured hangings and sculptures. Little is known of these because the furniture and hangings have generally been lost to decay, and any sculptures dispersed or replaced by later

19 Mosaic signed by Dioscurides of Samos, showing a scene of musicians from a play by the
Greek comic poet Menander. Second or early first century BC. 43 x 41cm. Naples Museum 9985.
Photograph Archaeological Superintendency Naples C5027 (ex 1195)

owners: the statuette of a dancing faun after which the House of the Faun was
named, for instance, may not have been part of the original furnishings. But we
can be sure that the 'Greekness' of the grand second-century mansions would
have been affirmed by textiles, statues and reliefs, either imported from Greece
or based upon Greek prototypes.

The last years of the second century and the early first century BC were
Pompeii's 'Regency period'. The city's elite built themselves residences of a
scale and distinction rarely repeated – within the city walls, at least – during the

following 150 years. And yet these richly appointed dwellings were not isolated from those of ordinary folk. They shared their *insulae* with the houses of artisans, with shops and with small apartments. Even the House of the Faun had shops set into its street-front – shops operated, no doubt, by freedmen or other dependents of the house owner. It was a pattern typical of Roman cities, and one which applied to Pompeii throughout its subsequent history.

3

THE ROMAN COLONY

The end of Pompeii's Samnite period came with the Social War of 91-89 BC. This is the name usually given to the struggle between Rome and a large number of her Italian allies who took up arms for a full share of the rights and privileges of Roman citizenship. The outcome of the war was that Rome won the victory but conceded the issue, offering her franchise first to those cities which had remained loyal, then to all the others as they came to heel. Pompeii was among the cities that joined the insurgents. It was captured after a lengthy siege in 89, and was eventually (by 84) admitted to the Roman commonwealth.[1] From now on, the language of official business in the city was Latin rather than Oscan, and the organs of local government took their titles from the Roman equivalents.

The siege of Pompeii has left its traces in the archaeological record. The last refurbishment of the city walls, carried out in *opus incertum* of black lava, has been dated to the late second century and may represent a precautionary measure in anticipation of conflict with Rome. It included the construction of a full complement of guard-towers, most of which probably replaced predecessors on the same foundations, but one of which – the so-called Torre di Mercurio (Tower of Mercury) – was on the site of the early gate at the north end of Via di Mercurio, now definitively closed (if it had not been closed before). The generous provision of towers on the northern defences reflects the fact that this was the most vulnerable part of the circuit; it was inevitable that the main force of an assault would fall here. Indeed, it is the north wall that shows the clearest signs of damage inflicted by the Roman artillery, while Region VI has yielded examples of the stone balls with which the city was bombarded, for example in the House of the Vestals (VI.1.7) and the House of the Labyrinth (VI.11.9-10) (*20*). A further relic of the siege may be the so-called *eítuns* ('soldiers on guard duty'?) inscriptions, notices in Oscan painted on street corners to instruct

20 Stone balls fired from catapults in the siege of 89 BC, found in the House of the Vestals (VI.1.7). *Photograph R.F.J. Jones*

the men of a given neighbourhood where to assemble in the event of attack.[2] These notices specifically refer to the towers, numbered I-XII in anti-clockwise sequence.

After the Social War Pompeii, unlike Stabiae, remained nominally self-governing. But in 80 BC, to ensure that it toed the line, it was given a colony of Roman veterans under the leadership of P. Cornelius Sulla, a younger relation of the dictator Sulla, who had commanded the army that had captured the city nine years earlier. Planting a veteran colony was a tried and tested policy during Rome's wars of expansion. It served the dual purpose of providing land and a livelihood for time-served soldiers and of establishing a focus of loyalty in newly subjugated regions. Normally, however, such colonies took the form of new towns founded on virgin sites. In Pompeii, the colony was imposed on a pre-existing city, and there were bound to be conflicts of interest between the new arrivals and the pre-existing population. The situation is reflected in the personalities of local politics. To judge from the known names, most of those elected to public office in the first years after colonisation were colonists and members of their families: the old Samnite clans that had held office in the preceding phase largely disappear from sight. The non-colonist population may effectively have been disfranchised for a time.[3] Echoes of difficulties at Pompeii

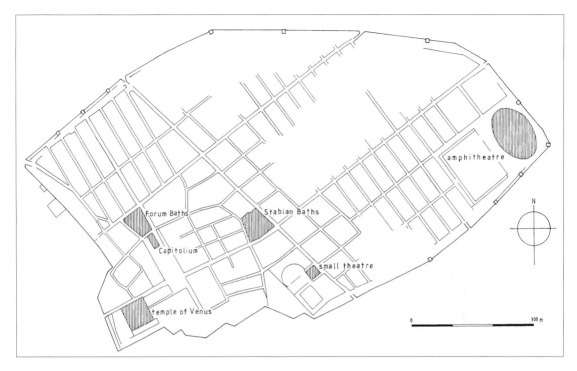

21 Plan showing buildings erected or modified in the colonial period. *Drawing R.J. Ling*

emerge from a speech delivered by the Roman orator and statesman Cicero in 62 BC. Defending the younger Sulla against a charge of being involved in a conspiracy against the government, he refers to disputes between the old residents and the colonists over the right to use a 'promenade' – perhaps the quadriportico of the putative *gymnasium* behind the theatre – and over matters connected with voting.[4] The dispute seems to have been referred to arbitration and settled, but it was doubtless not the only problem that arose.

The major mark made by the planting of the colony was upon the city's public architecture. An influx of Roman veterans with new social and cultural priorities demanded the provision of a number of buildings which were not previously available (*21*).

As in the preceding period – and as in all Greek and Roman cities – the new buildings were supervised, if not actually funded, by wealthy individuals on whom the duty fell as one of the conditions of holding public office. The survival of the dedicatory inscriptions with which the benefactors advertised their generosity enables us to link at least two buildings with the arrival of the colony. The first was the 'covered theatre' (*theatrum tectum*), the dedication of which names as founders two leading colonists, C. Quinctius Valgus and M. Porcius.[5] Built immediately to the east of the pre-existing large theatre,

22 Interior of the small (covered) theatre. Soon after 80 BC. *Photograph M. Nwokobia*

from which it is usually distinguished as the 'small theatre', this consisted of a semicircular auditorium uncomfortably fitted within a square shell of high walls that carried the timbers of a roof of remarkable span (approximately 26m, or 85ft) achieved without the aid of internal supports (*22*). The building is usually identified as an *odeion*, a Greek-style concert hall for musical performances and recitations, but it is difficult to believe that Roman ex-soldiers would have been much interested in promoting Greek culture in this way. A possible alternative function, suggested by Paul Zanker, was as an assembly chamber for meetings of the colonists.[6] The fact that this roofed auditorium was situated next to the large theatre does not necessarily imply that it, too, was intended for public entertainments. The position of both buildings was dictated by the convenience of a hill-slope in which their auditoria could be hollowed.

The second new building was the amphitheatre, financed by the same two colonists, Quinctius Valgus and Porcius, but at a slightly later date.[7] The official title was actually not *amphitheatron*, a Greek term used of such buildings only at a later date, but the Latin *spectacula*. This reflects the fact that the entertainments staged in the arena were of purely Roman type, the gladiatorial combats and wild-beast hunts which had evolved in central Italy, perhaps from games conducted at funerals, and whose brutality and bloodshed set them apart from the popular entertainments of the Greeks. The amphitheatre must have been designed therefore – initially at least – to respond to the demands of the Roman colonists rather than to those of the indigenous Pompeians: in this respect the wording of the dedicatory inscription, which states that the founders were acting 'for the honour of the colony' (*coloniai honoris caussa*) and 'dedicated the place to the perpetual use of the colonists' (*coloneis locum in perpetuom deder(unt))*, is surely significant. The building was sited away from other public buildings, in the eastern angle of the city. It is not certain whether, as often claimed, this was because the site in question was open land and thus available for development; recent excavations have indicated that the blocks in the eastern quarter were much more fully built up in their early stages (second century BC) than was later the case. Marginalising the amphitheatre had the advantage of keeping potentially rowdy crowds away from the city centre; at the same time, spectators from communities further up the Sarno valley, such as Nuceria, could be channelled in and out through the nearest city gates.

Other buildings of the colonial phase can be identified on historical or archaeological grounds. Pre-eminent was the temple of Venus. Venus was the patron deity of Sulla, and she acquired a similar role in relation to the colony, whose official title was Colonia Cornelia Veneria Pompeianorum ('Cornelia' after Sulla's family name, 'Veneria' after Venus). Her temple was constructed on a lofty platform at the south-west corner of the city, adjacent to the Marine Gate, where the goddess would be able to control and protect the route by which visitors arrived from the commercial port. It may well have been visible from the sea and thus have formed a conspicuous landmark, a kind of symbol of the city.

Of the buildings in the forum area, it is inconceivable that the colonists did not make changes to the dominant temple at the northern end (*23*). Even if this was already dedicated to Jupiter, there was probably now a rebuilding which laid emphasis on the Capitoline version of that god's cult, in which Jupiter shared honours with Juno and Minerva.[8] It may have been at this stage that the base for the cult statue within the temple was transformed into a three-chambered podium, while the whole building was radically re-designed and monumentalised. At the south end of the forum the Comitium, or voting enclosure, though perhaps begun in the pre-colonial period, was brought to completion in the first years of the colony.

Much of the building work of the colonists was carried out in a distinctive technique which we call 'quasi-reticulate'. This is a form of *opus incertum* in which the facing blocks are roughly standardised in size and shape to produce the effect almost of a network ('reticulate') of little square pieces set diagonally. Its advantages over normal *incertum* were its capacity for tighter fitting, which created a more homogeneous surface, and its streamlining of the building process. The material employed for the quasi-reticulate was black lava, but corners were rendered either in small rectangular blocks of Sarno stone and Nuceria tuff or, more distinctively, in courses of tiles laid in 'saw-tooth' triangular panels (*colour plate 5*).

23 North end of the forum, showing the remains of the Capitolium, with an arch at the left. In the foreground is a series of statue bases stripped of their marble veneer. *Photograph University of Manchester, Art History collection (Sommer 1208)*

The use of this technique permits us to assign another major building to the colonial phase – the Forum Baths (*24*). Situated in the block immediately to the north of the Capitoline temple, these represented a state-of-the-art project incorporating not just bathing facilities but also shops and upstairs apartments, and were clearly intended as an amenity for the general population, among whom the bathing habit had taken a firm hold, rather than for the colonists alone. Significantly, a pair of inscriptions which have been ascribed to the Forum Baths record the magistrates who supervised the work as operating at public expense (*ex pequnia publica*) rather than paying from their own pockets.[9] Evidently the Stabian Baths were now inadequate to the requirements of the city, and a new establishment was needed to relieve pressure on them. At the

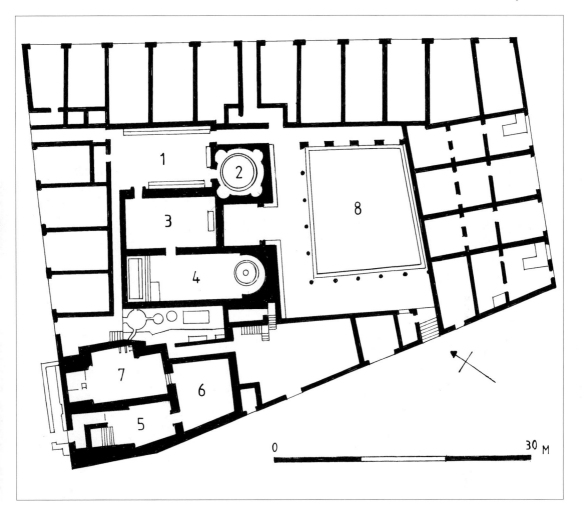

24 Plan of the Forum Baths (soon after 80 BC). 1: men's *apodyterium*; 2: men's *frigidarium* (originally *laconicum*); 3: men's *tepidarium*; 4: men's *caldarium*; 5: women's *apodyterium*; 6: women's *tepidarium*; 7: women's *caldarium*; 8: *palaestra. Drawing L.A. Ling*

same time the Stabian Baths themselves were modernised, as an inscription (*41*) reveals, by the addition of a *laconicum* (dry-heat room) and *destrictarium* (room for rubbing down after exercise) and by the reconstruction of the Baths *palaestra* and its porticoes.[10] The position of the new baths, like the old, was strategically chosen to benefit as large a slice of the urban population as possible. They took over the servicing of the northern and western quarters, leaving the Stabian Baths to cater for dwellers in the centre and east.

The impact of the colonists on Pompeii's public architecture was fundamental: they set the stamp on the transformation of the Hellenised Samnite city of the second century BC into the Roman city of the early Imperial period. What is much less clear is their influence on domestic architecture. Accommodation had to be found for several hundred veterans and their families, and one would expect to observe a major programme of house-building and rebuilding affecting the city in 80 BC; but no such phenomenon occurs.

It used to be believed by some – by H. Eschebach, for instance – that the first development of Pompeii's eastern quarter took place at this date and should be credited to the colonists;[11] but, as we have seen, the eastern development goes back to a much earlier phase in the city's history. If the colonists settled within the city walls, we can only assume that they did so by taking over existing houses whose owners had been killed or dispossessed.

Here some assistance may potentially be provided by the so-called 'Second Pompeian Style' of wall-painting. This style, which replaced the stucco relief and coloured blockwork of the First Style with a pictorial illusion of receding architecture executed entirely on a flat surface, seems to have been imported by the colonists. Early, simple versions are attested in the Capitolium and in the small theatre. Where similar decorations occur in private houses, one could argue that they were commissioned by the newly arrived colonists. A possible candidate for such a takeover is the House of the Labyrinth, where a monumental reconstruction of the peristyle quarter is thought to have been begun before the Social War and only completed, after a long suspension of operations, during the colonial phase.[12] Here, however, there is a problem. The Second Style wall-paintings in the House of the Labyrinth show a degree of complexity and elaboration impossible in the first years of the colony: even if we accept the highest chronology proposed for them, they are no earlier than the 60s, that is ten or more years after the colony's founding. There are hardly any Pompeian houses, in fact, that retain paintings assignable to the Second Style's earliest phases. If the colonists occupied properties within the walled area, we can only assume that the signs of their presence have been eradicated by rebuilding and redecoration in later times.

It is possible, however, that many of the colonists were settled outside the city, being given undeveloped land in the *territorium*. This would have had the advantage of reducing the risk of friction with the existing population; it would also have meant that the settlers did not have to travel back and forth from the city to cultivate their plots. Perhaps they formed the nucleus of the suburban administrative district later known as the Pagus Augustus Felix Suburbanus (the epithet 'Felix' was associated with Sulla and implies an origin in the colonial phase). Some support for extramural colonisation is provided, as F. Zevi has pointed out,[13] by the number of Second Style wall-decorations preserved in villas within the *territorium* – though most of these decorations are once again too late for the colony's initial phase.

The general trends in Pompeii's domestic architecture during the period following the planting of the colony are less easy to characterise, partly because of the dearth of wall-paintings datable to this period. There is no obvious sign of an abatement of luxury. Old mansions such as the House of the Faun retained their form and fittings, and new double-*atrium* houses were created by the joining of two houses which had originally been separate, e.g. the House of the Menander and its neighbour, the House of the Craftsman (I.10.4 and 7).[14] There was a continuing trend towards the building of peristyles and the opening of the *tablinum* and its adjacent rooms to face the garden. In the dwelling formed by merging the (later redivided) Houses of the Cryptoportico and of the Iliadic Shrine (I.6.2 and 4), where the land fell away to the rear, the householder took advantage of the situation to create a double-storeyed arrangement of a peristyle with a semi-subterranean corridor, the cryptoportico of the house name, providing a cool and shady ambulatory at a lower level.

An important development of this time was the domestic bath-suite, examples of which became more frequent after the middle of the first century. Often richly decorated with mosaic pavements, wall-paintings and stucco ceilings, these represented a conspicuous display of wealth. They would have consumed a steady supply of fuel and water, and their upkeep must have depended upon slaves to stoke the furnaces and fill the various tanks and basins. Heating came to be achieved not only by hypocausts but also by the use of special tiles, the so-called *tegulae mammatae* ('nippled tiles'), to create cavities within the walls. The hot air that circulated under the floors rose through these cavities and produced a radiant heat far more effective than that generated by a simple hypocaust. In some houses, notably those of the Menander and of the Cryptoportico, the source of the heat was an underlying domed oven of a type regularly associated with the baking of bread. The capacity to finance in-house bread production would have been a further factor setting the householder apart from most of his contemporaries, who would have had to buy loaves at the commercial bakeries.

In relation to detailed arrangements within houses, one of the most interesting innovations was a suite consisting of a large dining room or reception room with smaller rooms opening to the sides. The satellite rooms are clearly identified as bedchambers or rest-rooms by the presence of specially designated recesses for beds or couches. These suites generally face on to a peristyle or portico. An excellent example is at the rear of the peristyle in the House of the Labyrinth, where a grand reception room with internal columns round three sides – what the Roman architectural writer Vitruvius describes as a 'Corinthian *oecus*'[15] – is flanked on each side by a chamber with a single bed-alcove at the rear. Another format, found (for example) in the Villa of the Mysteries, combines a deep dining room with a single chamber containing a pair of alcoves, one at the rear and one in a side wall. The paired rooms are clearly linked functionally, the smaller one serving not merely as a bedroom but also as a kind of drawing room or office to which the master and selected guests could retire after a meal to conduct business.[16]

In regard to construction, the standard techniques were all based on mortared rubble. The 'quasi-reticulate' facings of the early colonial buildings evolved rapidly into true reticulate, with pieces cut mainly from Nuceria tuff though

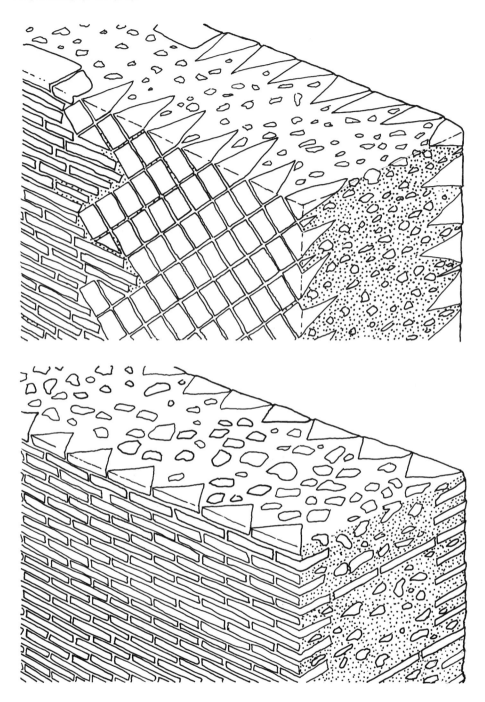

25 Diagram of construction in *opus reticulatum* (top) and brickwork (bottom). *Drawing after H. and R. Leacroft,* The Buildings of Ancient Rome *(1969), fig. 10*

sometimes in different materials (*colour plate 7*). These pieces, though presenting a grid of squares on the face of the wall, were actually pyramidal in shape: the base of the pyramid was on the surface, while the apex pointed inwards, keying into the mortar of the core (*25a*). Since Nuceria tuff could be cut with more precision than the other materials in common use, it facilitated the standardisation of shapes and sizes, and the best walls were beautifully regular in their finish. The same form of tuff, along with Sarno stone, was employed to make small building blocks similar in shape and size to modern house bricks which were laid in courses either as continuous facing (*opus vittatum*) or, more commonly, to frame windows and doorways, where panels of them engage tooth-like with facings of *incertum* or reticulate.

Among new materials, the yellow tuff from the Campi Phlegraei has already been mentioned. More significant is baked terracotta, in the form of bricks or tiles. This material, strong and fire-resistant, became increasingly common in structural roles during the first century BC. Like *vittatum*, it was used at first chiefly for cornering, as in the colonial buildings already described; but another function, going back to late second-century buildings such as the Basilica, was in the construction of columns. Courses of wedge-shaped pieces of brick, arranged radially, provided a cylindrical matrix which was then coated with stucco in imitation of work in marble (*26, colour plate 2*). The result was to substitute the old laborious technique of carving and fitting together carefully shaped stone drums by a much quicker and cheaper method, well suited to building the numerous peristyles that were needed during this period.

Roman bricks are thin compared with modern ones, and they were normally of triangular shape, laid (like the pyramidal pieces of reticulate) with one angle keying into the mortared core of the wall (*25b*). The first examples were obtained mainly by cutting roof tiles along the diagonal, but before long there were specially baked wall bricks (though still usually reduced from squares to triangles by diagonal cutting). Despite the cheapness of the technique in comparison with stone carving, bricks were evidently more expensive than rubble, if not also reticulate, facings, and were used sparingly. While most tiles and bricks were certainly produced on estates in the neighbourhood, others were imported from factories further afield, including northern Campania.

A technical development that gathered pace during the first century BC was the construction of vaulted ceilings. Concrete vaults were one of the major contributions of the Romans to the history of ancient architecture. First introduced in the second century BC for warehouses and other utilitarian buildings, they enabled builders to span much larger internal spaces than could be achieved with flat ceilings. This virtue, and the fact that they were stronger, more damp-resistant, and thus more durable than ceilings of timber, commended them especially in bath buildings. It was certainly in the public baths, notably the Stabian and the Forum Baths, that vault-construction made its first appearance at Pompeii. From here it spread to domestic architecture, being used, for example,

26 Detail of a brick column in the Large Palaestra (end of first century BC or beginning of first century AD). *Photograph J.B. Ward-Perkins*

in subterranean or supporting structures such as the cryptoporticoes of the Villa of the Mysteries and the House of the Cryptoportico.

The aesthetic of curved soffits was subsequently translated from concrete to other materials, and we find rooms in private bath-suites and alcoves in bedrooms spanned by 'suspended' vaults in which the curvature was supplied by a wooden armature to the underside of which was attached a mat of reeds or wattlework; this was then finished with a coat of plaster. Usually vaults constructed in this way were not fully semicircular – as were the barrel vaults of bath chambers or cryptoporticoes – but had shallower curves. Such segmental vaults were destined to become increasingly popular in the Imperial period, being used for reception rooms and dining rooms, sometimes combined with flat soffits to create dynamic rhythms distinguishing or privileging one part of a room – the area occupied by dining couches, for instance – in relation to another.

The early colonial period, as already hinted, saw the building or refurbishment of many villas in the countryside round Pompeii. One of them, the Villa of the Mysteries, named after the impressive figured mural in its most important room, was relatively close to the city and may well have required extensive repairs as a result of damage suffered in the siege of 89; at all events, most of the existing layout and decorations can be dated, in all probability, to a phase in the first two or three decades after the planting of the colony. Another finely appointed villa, conventionally named after a certain P. Fannius Synistor, is further north, at Boscoreale; its decorations suggest a slightly later date. Further to the west, the splendidly appointed villa 'of the Poppaei', decorated at much the same time as the one at Boscoreale, overlooked the sea at Oplontis (modern Torre Annunziata). Other villas, both grand and modest, have been excavated in various parts of the area to the north and east of the city. Almost all of them included working farms, with ample space afforded to the presses and vats for the production and storage of the wine which played a vital part in sustaining their owners' incomes.

These villas, unlike the town houses so far described, tended to be outward-looking. Several of them, including the Villa of Diomedes and the Villa of the Mysteries, were entered from the landward side, while the rear part was terraced out on substructures with panoramic rooms and ambulatories from which residents could enjoy a view of the coast and the sea. In some cases the arrangement of rooms followed the precepts laid down by Vitruvius for suburban villas, with the peristyle in front of, rather than behind, the *atrium*. This applies to the Villa of the Mysteries, where the working and storage rooms of the farm occupied the front range, convenient for access to the land (and reflecting the importance of agricultural production to the proprietor), while the peristyle came next, and the *atrium* and *tablinum*, surrounded by a complex of finely decorated living rooms, brought up the rear. The *atrium* was not here the visitor's first port of call, the focus of the house's public life, but the nucleus of a secluded quarter for the enjoyment of leisure in a beautiful natural setting.

The fact that the traditional town houses were inward-looking was a natural consequence of their urban environment. Partly for security reasons, partly to keep out the noise of the streets, they tended to present only small windows to the exterior – on the ground floor at least – and drew their light from the internal spaces of *atrium* and peristyle. Only when upper storeys were added – something that began to happen increasingly from this time onwards – did the new upstairs rooms, which were sufficiently high up to reduce the disturbance from traffic (and the risk of burglary), sometimes get larger windows overlooking the street. In the countryside, of course, no such constraints existed: the space around the villa and the potential for a panorama of the Bay of Naples encouraged the development of an outward-facing architecture. But during the course of the first century BC even the town began to acquire houses that exploited the view. The decommissioning of the city walls led to the construction of houses that spilled over the western and southern defences and descended the slopes outside in a series of terraces. Almost inconspicuous on the city side, these urban 'villas' included capacious rooms with big windows facing the coast, and their accumulation of space on two or three different levels, as in the so-called House of M. Fabius Rufus, produced a surface area scarcely inferior to that of the House of the Faun. The beginnings of this development, on the west side of the city, are dated around the middle of the century by Second Style mosaics and wall-paintings, but the presence of work in the Third Style, especially in the houses along the southern defences, show that it continued throughout the following period.

We may conclude with a few words on interior decoration. The Second Style marks a definitive shift of emphasis from the floors to the walls. While mosaic pictures continued to appear in the pavements of some prestigious rooms, there was an increasing tendency for paving to adopt all-over abstract patterns. A favourite motif at first was a regular scatter of fragments of coloured stones within a matrix of black or white tesserae. Later this gave way to geometric mosaics predominantly in black and white. The simplification of floor-decoration was intended to offset the new complexity of wall-painting. We have described this as presenting 'an illusion of receding architecture', but such a description does scant justice to the richness and imagination of some of the schemes that were now created. Using shading, perspective and foreshortening, the painters of the mid-first century BC dissolved the wall into a variety of planes, often with a screen of columns in the foreground, walls of coloured masonry in the middle ground, and glimpses of colonnades retreating into a shimmering distance behind (*colour plate 6*). The architecture thus depicted was solid and buildable, but it is doubtful whether any real buildings were so elaborately designed, for these structures played with the traditional vocabulary, cutting away the centre of a pediment, making arches spring from columns, and placing single-column forward projections in front of a colonnade. Moreover, the polychromy of the materials, which combined alabaster, porphyry and exotic marbles with gilded reliefs and inset gems, went far beyond the conventions of contemporary building. These decorations were intended to evoke the imagined luxury of eastern palaces or temples and thus give the domestic interior a regal and often mysterious grandeur. At the same time, there may have been some influence from scenery painted for the theatre: the fictive architecture often contains Greek actors' masks, and Vitruvius tells us that paintings 'in open spaces such as *exedrae*' reproduced 'stage-fronts in the tragic, comic, or satyric manner'.[17]

These paintings were, of course, not invented in Pompeii. They were imported ready-made from the houses and villas of Roman grandees, who may have commissioned them out of a desire to cultivate the semblance of living in the style of Hellenistic kings. Like many later fashions, they passed into the repertoire of the local aristocracies and, given the extraordinary conditions of Pompeii's burial, are known to us chiefly from the 'second-hand' versions. Their importance is as evidence of what was going on in the higher echelons of Roman-Italian society. In this perspective they can be seen as inaugurating a mode of *trompe l'oeil* architectural painting which was unprecedented in domestic wall-painting but which subsequently evolved towards ever more colourful and revolutionary compositions – compositions which are attested by examples from the succeeding phases of Pompeii's existence.

4

THE EARLY EMPIRE

The half century following the planting of the Sullan colony at Pompeii coincided with the final years of the Roman Republic. The various social, economic and administrative problems created by the expansion of Roman power to embrace most of the Mediterranean basin led to civil wars which were resolved only by the victory of Octavian over Mark Antony at the battle of Actium in 31 BC. Octavian, who took the title of Augustus in 27 BC, set about building a new order based on an administrative structure of long-serving professional officials and maintained by an army stationed permanently in key frontier areas. Though careful to avoid any open display of absolutism and working ostensibly within constitutional formulae, he nonetheless consolidated his personal position as first citizen, or *princeps* – a kind of Orwellian 'first among equals' – to the point that, by the time of his death in AD 14, the Roman world had moved so far along the path to monarchy that there was no realistic prospect of turning back. Augustus was succeeded by his stepson Tiberius, and the first imperial dynasty (the Julio-Claudians) came into existence.

The reign of Augustus provided a period of stability and security buttressed by an ideological programme which emphasised concepts such as the revival of traditional religious and moral values. In Pompeii, as in hundreds of other communities, prominent local citizens sought to express their gratitude to the new regime, and in some cases to secure their personal advancement, by sponsoring building projects which honoured the emperor or promoted his ideals. A good example was the erection by M. Tullius, a leading magistrate of the last decades of the first century BC, of the temple dedicated to Fortuna Augusta, one of various cults which grew up round the emperor and his tutelary spirits. Tullius had received honours from the emperor, and the building of the temple was a statement of his loyalty. Moreover, its location at a busy crossroads two streets north of the forum was well suited to advertise the cult and, with it,

27 Statue of M. Holconius Rufus, set up in the street outside the Stabian Baths. He wears military dress to indicate his status as a military tribune. Ht 2.02m. Naples Museum 6233. *Photograph Ward-Perkins collection*

the munificence and political correctness of the donor. The land on which the temple was built formed part of Tullius' private property, and he was fortunate to be able to turn this circumstance to advantage.[1]

Another prominent citizen of the Augustan period was M. Holconius Rufus, who at various stages held all the chief posts in the local administration, acted as a priest of the imperial cult and, like Tullius, was rewarded by the emperor with a grant of the honorary title of military tribune (*27*). He too was active in public building. During his third tenure of the duovirate (the city's chief executive office), i.e. not long before 2 BC, the year of his fourth tenure, he and his fellow duovir C. Egnatius Postumus built a wall which blocked light from the windows of houses adjacent to the sanctuary of Apollo. An inscription found in the sanctuary records the compensation paid to the householders who were affected.[2] It is normally believed that the layout of the precinct, with its rigid axial planning and colonnaded courtyard, goes back to the second century BC, but recent trial excavations have yielded dating evidence that points to building activity in the late first century BC.[3] Since the wall which impinged upon neighbouring properties was clearly the west precinct boundary, and since this is an integral part of the overall plan, it seems that Holconius and his colleague were responsible for a radical rebuilding and enlargement which resulted in the suppression of an early street along the west side. In either case their concern for the cult of Apollo acquires added significance from the fact that Apollo was Augustus' patron deity. It was natural to demonstrate allegiance to the new regime by promoting the interests of its leader's favourite god.

Another leading benefactor of the Augustan period was the public priestess Mammia, who paid for the sanctuary of the Genius of Augustus.[4] The provenance of the inscription which records her dedication is uncertain, but it has been plausibly linked with one of the buildings on the east side of the forum, the so-called Temple of Vespasian (*28*). If this is correct, Mammia owned (or bought) the plot in question because she, like M. Tullius, records that the temple was built not just at her own expense but on her own land. An Augustan date for the building is supported by the imagery of the reliefs on the altar which stood in front of the temple (*44*).[5] We may, therefore, suspect that the monumentalisation of the forum's east front, with the old shops and workshops being replaced by large public complexes, began in Augustan times.

Elsewhere in the city M. Holconius Rufus appears again, this time with his son (or brother) Holconius Celer, another leading figure in the imperial cult and the local administration, carrying out major alterations to the large theatre: they funded a *crypta* (probably an anular corridor which supported an extra tier of seating at the back of the auditorium), *tribunalia* (the boxes constructed over the side-passages, or *parodoi*, which led to the area in front of the stage), and the *theatrum* (presumably the seating in general).[6] Apparently the Holconii not only enlarged and refurbished the auditorium but also, by adding *tribunalia*, completed the conversion of the theatre from its old Hellenistic form, in which

28 Temple of the Genius of Augustus (traditionally identified as the temple of Vespasian): view of the interior. *Photograph R.J. Ling 113/8*

the auditorium was separate from the stage-building, to something approaching the standard Roman type in which the two elements were unified in a single structure. Investing in civic theatres was a widespread cultural phenomenon of the reign of Augustus, for which the emperor himself set a precedent by his dedication of the monumental Theatre of Marcellus in Rome.

A further major building of the Augustan period cannot, for lack of evidence, be connected with any individual benefactors but fits the same pattern of conformance to government ideology: the so-called Large Palaestra (*colour plate 8*), situated next to the amphitheatre. As already stated, this was a *campus* (training ground) for the military corps of upper-class youths which Augustus promoted as part of a policy of producing model citizens and supporters of his regime. When not in use for drills and other displays, it may have been open to the general public as a *gymnasium* or simply a pleasant intramural open space, analogous to the monumental *porticus*, such as the Porticus of Octavia and the Porticus of Livia, which the emperor created (in continuance of a Republican tradition) in the capital. It was provided with a central swimming pool and planted with plane trees whose estimated age at the time of the eruption is the chief argument for an Augustan date. The importance of the Campus is attested by the fact that the space was obtained by suppressing six blocks of the pre-existing street-grid.

29 Water tower and
fountain at the junction
of Via Stabiana and Via
dell'Abbondanza (north-
west corner of I.4).
*Photograph M. Thatcher
(Ward-Perkins collection)*

Recent excavations have yielded traces of early properties which must have
been bought or expropriated. One reason for placing the Campus in the eastern
part of the city may have been that this quarter was less densely populated than
others, so that the cost of the development and the degree of disruption that it
caused were less than they would have been elsewhere.

While the buildings so far mentioned were the result of local initiative, a final
contribution of the Augustan age to Pompeii's public landscape was apparently
due to government investment. The city may already have obtained its first
running water before the end of the Republic,[7] but this was now superseded
by what was certainly a much more systematic and reliable supply, furnished by
a branch of the aqueduct constructed by Augustus' minister Agrippa to service
the fleet at Misenum. In improving the quality of life in the city the provision
of fresh water was of immeasurable importance. Its chief visual impact was in
the creation of two new streetside features (*29*): the series of water towers which

regulated the pressure of flow from the distributing tank (*castellum aquae*) at the Vesuvius Gate and the public fountains which were located at street corners to service the needs of those residents of neighbouring blocks who did not have water piped into their own homes. The arrival of running water will also have led to improvements in the functioning of the public baths. The dedication of a new wash basin in the Forum Baths, dated to AD 3/4, may have been one consequence of it.[8] The building of the Suburban Baths outside the Marine Gate may have been another.

The reign of Augustus was a seminal phase in the history of Pompeii's public landscape, but it merely marked the beginning of a development which continued under Augustus' successors. Sometimes it is difficult to know whether buildings should be dated to the Augustan or Julio-Claudian periods. On the east side of the forum, for instance, the building funded by Eumachia contained references to Augustan propaganda, including replicas of the statues of Aeneas and Romulus from the Forum of Augustus in Rome, but its dedicatory inscriptions, which record that Eumachia constructed the building in her own name and that of her son, M. Numistrius Fronto, and dedicated it to Concordia Augusta and Pietas, fit a period early in the reign of Tiberius, and especially the years AD 22-24, when there was emphasis on the close relations between the emperor and his mother Livia, and concepts such as concord and filial devotion (*pietas*) would have been in fashion. A post-Augustan date is supported by details of the building's Third Style wall-paintings, known from nineteenth-century drawings.[9] The Macellum, the principal food market, at the north-east corner of the forum, is not securely dated and it too could belong in its present form to the Julio-Claudian phase. Its southern neighbour, usually called the Temple of the Public Lares but identified by Zanker, plausibly, as a sanctuary for the imperial cult, may have been added even later, perhaps not before the city's last years.[10]

The monumental development of the forum may, therefore, have continued through the early Imperial period. Other buildings around it, such as the vegetable market to the north of the sanctuary of Apollo, and the three municipal buildings on the south side, could also have taken their final form at this time. What is striking is the piecemeal nature of the development, which produced façades on different alignments and plans with shifts of orientation. The whole picture is one of individual initiative, in which leading magistrates vied with each other to make an impact upon the urban landscape in this most prestigious area of the city.

But, as time went on, there was an effort to unify this heterogeneous architecture. Although there had been an early attempt to build a colonnade round the piazza, dated on the basis of an inscription to the 80s BC (*9*),[11] this may never have got much further than the southern end. Work was carried forward and largely completed during the Imperial period (*colour plate 9*), substituting a superior material, limestone, for the volcanic tuff of the original project. Similar improvements were made in the paving. At the same time, the honorary statues which had proliferated and been distributed in a somewhat haphazard fashion were apparently tidied up, the equestrian figures being lined up in front of the western colonnade, the standing figures perhaps set inside the eastern, while at the southern end was installed a symmetrical grouping of monumental bases which must have carried statues of particularly important personages, perhaps Augustus and members of the ruling house. A centrally located base towards the northern end is thought by Zanker to have carried an altar of the imperial cult,[12] but a statue of one of the emperors is again a possibility. To left and right of the temple of Jupiter the forum space was defined by a pair of monumental arches (*23*; cf. *37*), though at a later stage, probably between AD 23 and 29, the one at the right was replaced by another set further back to allow a clear view of the colonnade in front of the Macellum. Further north a smaller arch, dating perhaps to the reign of Caligula (AD 37-41), was built across the entrance to Via di Mercurio, providing a visual focus to the colonnaded street behind the Tiberian arch.

The monumentalisation of the forum and main streets fits with a trend which was common to cities of the early Imperial period. Formal axial planning, spaces defined by colonnades, the use of superior building materials – all were fundamental to the new urban landscape. From the Fora of Caesar and Augustus in Rome, they were disseminated to the new colonies of northern Italy and the provinces and served as models to be emulated by old cities too.

For the development of Pompeii's domestic architecture in the early Empire we are dependent, as in the previous period, on reading clues which indicate the relevant structural changes within houses which had existed from the second century BC or earlier. Once again, the chief dating criterion is the mode of interior decoration associated with such changes, and difficulty is caused by the effects of later alterations which have destroyed the relevant evidence. However, it seems that the Augustan and Julio-Claudian periods saw an increasing tendency to the construction of upper storeys, whether entered directly from the street or from within existing residences; there were also developments in the layout and fittings of the traditional *atrium* house which may reflect changing patterns in the social functioning of different rooms.

The addition of upper storeys logically implies an increase of population which exerted pressures on space: there were not enough rooms available at ground level, so owners were forced to build upwards. This is clearly the implication of the apartments inserted within the *atrium* house, an architectural type which was ill-suited to upward growth. They were invariably piecemeal developments and involved awkward compromises, with the lowering of ceilings in ground-floor rooms and the introduction of clerestoreys above the *atrium* roof. In such cases we are looking at desperate measures to cope with enlarged households and perhaps especially to accommodate the families of slaves who had acquired their freedom. Similar circumstances may help to explain another phenomenon of the time: the conversion of shops in the front rooms of houses into independent units. So long as these shops were linked by a doorway to the *atrium*, we can probably assume that they were operated by the householder through the agency of a freedman or other dependent; but the closure of the connecting doorway implies that they became independent businesses, run perhaps by the same freedmen, who would now have paid rent for the use of the premises.

Pressures on space do not, however, appear to have been uniform throughout the city. In the eastern part, so far as we can judge from the excavated areas, many houses were suppressed or reduced in size. The possible removal of private properties to make way for the Campus has already been mentioned. In addition to that, several of the small 'Hoffmann' houses in Region II and in the easternmost *insulae* of Region I were taken over by their neighbours and demolished to provide space for vineyards and market gardens.[13] The south-east quarter thus saw an expansion in green areas. It is possible that this trend may have been linked with the more intensive use of space in the central and western zones and along main streets such as Via dell'Abbondanza: householders in the south-east quarter perhaps felt impelled, for one reason or another, to sell up and move closer to the commercial hub of the city. But our knowledge of social and economic conditions is too tenuous to pursue such speculation, and the issue is best left open.

The main changes in the layout and furnishing of the *atrium* house focused round the changing role of the *atrium* itself. Traditionally the central reception area of the house, and associated with the political self-presentation of the old elite, expressed in such institutions as the cult of the ancestors and the *salutatio* – the ritual morning call paid by clients to their patrons – this tended to acquire a less formal character, with the introduction of marble furnishings, statuary and even water-pouring elements, such as a satyr decanting water from a wineskin into an adjacent basin.[14] The *atrium* was beginning to become a place where owners made a show of their material wealth, often in a colourful and light-hearted manner that ill suited the hall's connotations of sober grandeur. There are even some houses, such as that of Paquius Proculus and the House of the Boar I, where the traditional type of *atrium* paving, dark-coloured and economically decorated, was replaced by eye-catching black and white mosaics featuring not just geometric patterns but also figures (*30*). In the context of what went before, the effect would have been startling, and conservative viewers would surely have been shocked.

Along with a more ostentatious treatment of the *atrium* went an increased emphasis upon reception suites opening from the peristyle. Rather than simply turning the *tablinum* and any adjacent dining rooms to face the rear, house owners now began to create purpose-built suites off the peristyle's side or rear porticoes. These often featured a particularly large festal dining room or reception room, flanked by symmetrical smaller chambers. It has been suggested, plausibly, by J.-A. Dickmann that the great dining room came to take over some of the functions of the old *atrium*, and that this signified a subtle change in the nature of patronage

30 View into the House of P. Paquius Proculus (I.7.1) showing the mosaic paving of the *atrium* (late first century BC or early first century AD). Such showy floor decorations conflicted with the traditional sobriety of this space. *Photograph R.J. Ling 100/10*

and in the type of house owner.[15] The formal audience in the *atrium*, attended by clients drawn from a wide social spectrum, lost ground to more informal and more selective receptions focused in the dining room. This development went hand in hand with the decline of the old ruling families and the rise to political prominence of a new class of self-made men who had no influential ancestry and to whom the old associations of the *atrium* were less meaningful. Unencumbered by any firm attachment to the traditional patron-client relationship, with its system of formal visits and mutual obligations, they cultivated the lifestyle of the rich man's country villa, in which favour was courted and bestowed through a nexus of 'friendships', through exchanges of gifts, and through invitations to dinner parties where the host sought to impress his guests with the lavishness of his entertainment and the luxury of his furnishings.

The same factors explain the tendency, among many of Pompeii's householders, to foster the ambience of a country estate. A desire to recreate a villa in miniature within an urban context perfectly responded to the aspirations of the new upwardly mobile classes who had never owned the real thing.[16] Among the most obvious tokens of villa imitation was the ornamental garden enlivened with sculptures and water displays. True villas such as the sumptuous mansion at Oplontis had space for great tree-lined pools and avenues flanked by life-sized statues – ancient forerunners of the parks at Versailles or Nymphenburg. In urban Pompeii these things were reproduced 'on the cheap'. The statues were reduced to crowded assemblages of small bronze Cupids, marble basins and pillars, statuettes of animals and hanging discs, all set amid the shrubs and flowers of a comparatively tight peristyle garden, as in the Houses of the Gilded Cupids and of the Vettii (*74*). Water features were limited, usually, to a cascade over steps in a fountain niche or a jet pouring from the mouth of a dolphin or the like into a basin. Only in one or two exceptional cases, notably the garden of the House of D. Octavius Quartio, was there space for a landscape of canals spanned by bridges and pavilions and skirted by shady walkways (*31*).

However cramped and undiscriminating these gardens seem to us, to their owners they clearly represented an important status symbol. A considerable financial investment must have gone into creating them. Not only was there the cost of purchasing the bronze and marble *objets d'art*, but the water for fountains

31 Garden of the House of D. Octavius Quartio, also known as the House of Loreius Tiburtinus (II.2.2), showing decorative pavilions and water features. *Photograph Alinari 43280*

had to be piped from the city mains, a service which presumably entailed the payment of some kind of standing charge to the authorities. That having a private supply of running water was expensive is indicated by the fact that some large houses made do without one, continuing to depend, as they had before the construction of the aqueduct, upon the collection of rainwater.

The ornamental gardens were often made to appear larger than they were by illusionistic techniques, and especially by the painting of enclosing walls, or of the parapets which became increasingly common between the columns of peristyles, with shrubs and marble basins that reflected the real ones in front of them. In this way the limited spaces available in smaller houses – many of them little more than backyards – could be visually extended and enhanced. In some cases the walls were opened up with panoramic paintings of landscapes or harbour scenes, aping the real vistas that villa owners (such as the younger Pliny in the early second century, or indeed those Pompeians who constructed 'urban villas' over the city's disused western and southern walls) could admire from their windows. A favourite theme was the *paradeisos*, a landscape populated by exotic animals (*colour plate 10*) – a clear reference to the safari parks that had been a feature of the estates of Hellenistic kings and that were imitated by the villa-owning grandees of Roman Italy. All this gave the Pompeian householders a sense of sharing in a culture of luxury and privilege that they could never experience in reality. The gardens and their decorations were always designed, moreover, to be seen to best effect. Reception rooms had broad doorways to take advantage of views into them. Often a particularly eye-catching element, a fountain for example, was strategically placed at the focus of a sightline, whether this ran from the couch of the guest of honour in a dining room or from the house's principal entrance (*63*).

In terms of building materials and techniques, the early Imperial period saw the same tendency towards superior and more showy choices as in house and garden furnishings. Brick facings became more common, not just for columns and door frames but sometimes for whole façades, as in the Temple of the Genius of Augustus (*32*) and in the commemorative arches north of the forum (*23*). More significant was the use of marble veneer. The opening, during the first century BC, of the quarries at Luni, north of Pisa, meant that a convenient source of fine white marble, a material hitherto imported from the Aegean, became available in Italy itself. This transformed the history of Roman architecture. In Rome itself Augustus boasted, somewhat hyperbolically, that he had converted a city of mud brick into one of marble; and it certainly became normal for the more prestigious buildings to have columns and entablatures made from this material (rather than limestone), and for the main walls to be, at least, veneered with plaques of it. The same was true in lesser measure of the works carried out by public benefactors in the cities of Italy and the western provinces. Thus at Pompeii the brickwork of the temple of the Genius of Augustus was masked by a coating of marble sheets,[17] while the reliefs of its Augustan altar (*44*) were

32 Brick-faced wall of the temple of the Genius of Augustus with remains of a mortar surfacing prepared for a decoration of marble veneer. *Photograph R.J. Ling 68/7A*

carved on slabs of the same material. The ready availability of marble also helps to explain the proliferation of marble statuettes in Pompeii's houses and gardens.

It was not just white but also coloured marble that came into play under the early Empire. The settled conditions imposed by Augustus' victory and the centralised bureaucracy that resulted from his reforms promoted trade in exotic materials from all parts of the Mediterranean basin. It is likely that a desire for coloured marbles for use in the emperor's building programmes led, in the time of Tiberius, to many of the quarries being put under direct government supervision. But this did not prevent the materials from passing into widespread use in civic and domestic contexts all over the Empire. The yellow and pink *giallo antico* from Chemtou in Tunisia, the purple-veined *pavonazzetto* from Docimium in Asia Minor, the purple, black and white *africano* from Teos, also in Asia Minor, and ultimately the purple-red porphyry from Mons Porphyrites (Djebel Dokhan) in Egypt – these and many others reached Pompeii. Here the surviving evidence comes mainly from paving. A favourite technique was a scattering of small pieces – many of them clearly offcuts from the workshops of the marble-workers who prepared larger sheets for wall veneers in public buildings – within a matrix of mortar or tessellation. But, as time went on, there was an increasing fashion for pavements with *emblemata*, or even whole surfaces, composed of different coloured pieces carefully cut and joined to form geometric patterns. This so-called 'sectile' technique was evidently a hallmark of luxury and was confined chiefly to public buildings; where it occurred in houses and villas, its role was generally to privilege the main reception rooms.

A further development of the early Imperial period was the increased monumentalisation of the architecture of death. As in all Greek and Roman cities, Pompeii's cemeteries lay outside the city gates.[18] Series of tombs have been excavated outside the north-west gate, running along the road to Herculaneum, which has consequently become known as Via dei Sepolcri (Street of the Tombs), and outside the Nuceria Gate, where they line a road which runs parallel to the walls (*8*). Further tombs have been revealed outside the Vesuvius, Nola and Stabiae Gates, but here excavations have not been carried beyond the first few monuments in the cemetery.

Prior to the planting of the Roman colony, burials seem to have been relatively simple, with bodies interred in stone- or tile-lined cists or merely laid in the earth. After the arrival of the colonists, the standard means of disposal of the dead became cremation, and the first monumental tombs began to be built. Inscriptions recorded the name of the deceased for the benefit of passers-by – though, in most cases, simply as a statement of ownership rather than to seek advertisement. Fittingly, one of the earliest monuments known, situated outside the Herculaneum Gate, is that of M. Porcius, one of the leaders of the colony and joint builder of the small theatre and the amphitheatre. Another is the Tomb of the Garlands, named after the decoration of its exterior walls (the identity of its owner is not preserved).

But it is to the Augustan period that the first major surge in tomb construction must be dated. One of the notable features of this time, recorded in the surviving inscriptions, is the granting by the city to its prominent citizens of a burial plot on public land. We are particularly well informed because many of the plots in question were allocated in the *pomerium*, the 100ft (30.50m) wide strip of land immediately outside the walls,[19] and it is in this zone that excavation has been most complete. There was a tradition, supported by law, that the *pomerium* of Roman cities should be kept free of tombs, but it seems that in Pompeii this embargo began to be relaxed in the late-Republican period, as the local council sought space for monuments in honour of those who had rendered the city distinguished service. Clusters of such monuments appear outside the Herculaneum, Nola and Stabiae Gates.

Among these memorials a characteristically Pompeian species, largely exclusive to Augustan and Tiberian times, is the semicircular bench, or *schola*. Carved of volcanic tuff, with a winged lion's paw forming a terminal armrest at each end, this displayed an inscription with details of the citizen commemorated. It was a more elaborate counterpart of the modern commemorative seat, serving the

33 Schola of Mammia in the Street of the Tombs. Early first century AD. In the background are three reconstructed columns of a later monument, the so-called Tomb of the Istacidii. *Photograph German Archaeological Institute Rome 77.2170*

dual purpose of honouring the dead and providing a public amenity. The *schola* decreed for Mammia (*33*), the builder of the temple of the Genius of Augustus, was one of a pair outside the Herculaneum Gate, and it still offers a resting place for modern visitors: many famous tourists, including Goethe, have sat there to admire the view of the Sorrento peninsula. A similar bench outside the Stabiae Gate commemorated M. Tullius, the builder of the temple of Fortuna Augusta. Whether such *scholae* always functioned as tombs, is uncertain: the deceased could have been buried within the semicircular space enclosed by the bench or under a column or statue set immediately behind it, but in some cases the monument may have been a cenotaph for a person buried elsewhere.

Whether or not the plot was donated by the city or bought by the owner and the bereaved relatives, the remaining tombs tend to conform to a number of principal architectural types. Among the more common was the altar-tomb, in which a block in the shape of a monumental altar was mounted on a high podium; this could be solid, in which case it presumably marked the spot of a burial in the ground beneath, but in other cases there was an internal chamber (usually entered from a doorway at the side or rear so as to be less obvious) with wall niches for cinerary urns. Each niche served a different member of the owner's family or dependents. More ambitious were the double-storeyed monuments, in which a high podium with or without a burial chamber carried an upper element in the form of a columnar pavilion or rotunda. These included the most conspicuous edifices of the necropolis. They frequently exhibited statues of the dead between the columns. Another variant form punctuates the podium with a deep arched recess at the centre. Grandest of all among the known monuments is that of Eumachia, whose expenditure on public architecture is demonstrated by the forum building that bears her name. She was commemorated by an apse-fronted tomb erected on a spacious terrace. The façade would have been articulated with columns and niches containing statues, producing an effect analogous to that of monumental fountain buildings.

In many cases the monuments described were independent structures, but in others they were set within, or flanked by, walled enclosures, where additional burials could be placed in the ground. Some families opted simply for a burial enclosure, enhanced by a crowning pediment on the front wall but otherwise architecturally undistinguished. Where burials were in the ground, their positions were generally marked by a type of gravestone peculiar to the Sarno valley in which a rounded finial gave the effect of a head on shoulders (*34*); the idea may have been in some sense to imbue the slab with the spirit of the deceased whose name was cut upon it.

The lavishness or otherwise of funerary structures naturally depended on the means of the family. But not all those who could afford to build an expensive monument chose to do so: elite families in particular often renounced this option, regarding statues in the forum as a more appropriate and conspicuous form of memorial.[20] Some of the grander tombs belonged not to the municipal aristocracy but to well-off freedmen, who were eager to flaunt their achievements. Poorer families, needless to say, had to make do with simple monuments – miniature free-standing niches, for example. Slaves and other dependents would have places in communal tomb-chambers or burial enclosures built by their owners or patrons. For those who had no families to pay for their burials the city had to provide communal plots. Ironically, one such is known outside the Nola Gate in the same pomerial space that was otherwise set aside for monuments to the 'great and good'.[21]

One of the trends of later funerary architecture is the increasing showiness of certain tombs. Just as Pompeii's *nouveaux riches* adorned their houses with water displays, mosaics and garden sculptures, so did the same people decorate their tombs with paintings and reliefs. Many of the monuments in question belong to

34 Tombstones in the form of rudimentary portrait busts. Burial enclosure of L. Barbidius Communis (necropolis outside the Nuceria Gate). *Photograph J.B. Ward-Perkins*

the last years of the city and should properly be dealt with in the next chapter, but it is convenient to mention them here. A good example is the monument constructed in the Via dei Sepolcri by Naevoleia Tyche for herself and her husband, the prominent freedman and *augustalis* (member of the fraternity that administered the imperial cult) C. Munatius Faustus. The crowning altar celebrates Faustus' services and honours both by means of a long funerary inscription and through the medium of carved reliefs. Beneath the inscription we see men, women and children receiving a distribution of corn or flour paid for by Faustus (*35*), and on the left side is a representation of the ceremonial double theatre seat (*bisellium*) which, as the inscription informs us, had been granted to Faustus by the council in recognition of his public munificence. On the right side is a relief of a ship, emblematic no doubt of the maritime trade to which Faustus owed his wealth. A similar monument commemorates another freedman and *augustalis*, C. Calventius Quietus, who had also received the privilege of a *bisellium*; here the *bisellium* is depicted on the altar's front face while the sides carry wreaths referring to Quietus' role as a priest of the imperial cult.

The emphasis of all these depictions is on the life and achievements of those commemorated. There is none of the spiritual content that we would expect of memorials in a modern cemetery. Another tomb, perhaps that of N.

35 Detail of reliefs on the crowning altar of the tomb of Naevoleia Tyche, Street of the Tombs. The bust above the dedicatory inscription must represent Naevoleia Tyche's husband, C. Munatius Faustus. Below is a scene of slaves shovelling corn or flour into the baskets of a queue of men, women and children, evidently a dole funded by Faustus, *c.* AD 60. *Photograph German Archaeological Institute Rome 77.2085*

Festius Ampliatus, is covered with stucco reliefs commemorating the events in a gladiatorial show which the dead man had sponsored.[22] The monument of C. Vestorius Priscus, a young aedile who appears to have died in office, contained paintings showing him in the doorway of his house, sitting in judgement or receiving clients, and entertaining friends to a drinking party; there were also references to a show that he had staged in the amphitheatre, and an illustration of the family silver (*colour plate 11*).[23] In Priscus' tomb, the paintings were inside an enclosure and not visible to the general public, which would have seen only stucco reliefs of conventional Bacchic figures on the crowning altar and on little turrets at the corners of the enclosure walls. But in all cases the chief concern of these citizens and their families was clearly with their careers and civic responsibilities. The inscriptions record name, status, honours, sometimes the age of the deceased (especially where death had occurred at an early age, preventing the realisation of a true potential), and sometimes the name of a widow or parent who had set up the monument. None shows any signs of religiosity, nor are there many hints of the poignant sympathies revealed by some other epitaphs of the Roman world.

To turn from architecture and architectural ornament to interior decoration, the reign of Augustus marked a change from the grand illusionistic architecture of Second Style wall-painting to the elegant restraint of the Third. Vestiges of columnar structures continued to appear at the centre of the wall and in the upper zone, but they were now reduced to beanpole proportions and any residual perspective became perfunctory, if not illogical (*colour plate 12*). Particularly characteristic was the central pavilion or *aedicula* with a pair of flimsy columns, basically white but adorned with little collars and other decorative motifs in red, blue or purple, which supported a polychrome entablature. This edifice presented no true sense of volume or reality: its function was simply to serve as a frame for what was the dominant motif of the decoration: a large picture panel. The central picture (*colour plate 13*) was in many respects the defining element of the Third Style. Generally featuring a subject from Greek mythology, often with the figures reduced in scale and set in a vast landscape of beetling crags and twisted trees, it was clearly intended to give the impression of one of the 'old masters' painted on wooden panels which wealthy collectors of the late Republic had imported from Greece. The compositions of the pictures may well have been derived from those of famous masterpieces, but the fresco painters who produced these 'replicas' evidently worked from rough sketches or from workshop traditions and freely adapted settings and colours, introduced extra figures, or even modified the basic components. Such modifications did not concern the bourgeois patron. What mattered was the effect of a picture gallery that the completed scheme conveyed. The mythological pictures were another way of emulating the trappings of aristocratic grandeur, while at the same time demonstrating that the householder was *au fait* with the classical myths which were the focus of the literary and artistic culture of the age.

The rest of the decorative scheme was subservient to the central picture. Here the play of advancing and receding forms fundamental in the Second Style gave way to broad areas of plain colouring: red, black, or occasionally the more expensive pigments blue or green (*colour plate 31*). Such divisions as occurred took the form of bands adorned with miniature detail (heart shapes, lyres, birds and so forth) exquisitely drawn and rendered in brilliant polychromy. But, as time went on, there returned a hankering after the old three-dimensional effects. The architectural elements, while remaining slender and unreal, acquired more volume and a more coherent perspective; window-like openings containing receding colonnades appeared between the fields in the main zone of the decoration; the central picture panels gradually shrank in size, becoming more nearly square rather than vertical oblongs. Within the pictures, the figure scenes, which had been relatively cool and two-dimensional in effect, even when set in landscape, became more dramatic and colouristic, with violent movement and strong contrasts between light and shade. All this announced the birth of the last of the phases of Pompeian painting, the so-called Fourth Style, to be considered in the next chapter.

5

THE LAST YEARS

In the years around AD 50 there was little sign of the troubles to come. At Rome the aging emperor Claudius, brought to power unexpectedly following the assassination of his nephew Caligula in 41, had for all his muddleheadedness and physical infirmities presided over a phase of stable and effective government. At Pompeii, though social changes were in motion, with the rise to prominence of new families, including some of freedman stock, and with increasing pressures on living space in parts of the city, there was certainly no crisis threatening the established order. Within less than 15 years everything had changed.

Claudius' disastrous marriage to his niece Agrippina sowed the seeds of his ruin. On his death in 54, poisoned (it was said) by his wife, he was succeeded by her son of an earlier marriage, whom she had persuaded him to adopt, the 16-year-old Nero. The new emperor had little understanding of, or interest in, the everyday business of government, and in due course, after a quiet phase during which the administration was in the hands of able and responsible ministers, he began to reveal the less savoury side of his character. The murder of his mother in 59 and the rise to power of sycophantic and unscrupulous advisors led to increasingly erratic behaviour which provoked conspiracies and a climate of fear among the upper classes. Ultimately, in 68, the armies rose in revolt and Nero was overthrown, bringing to an end the Julio-Claudian dynasty and ushering in a new round of civil war.

The reign of Nero saw the violent interruption of regular life and tranquillity at Pompeii. After generations of obscurity the small Campanian city hit the headlines, first because of a riot in its amphitheatre in 59, and secondly as the result of a devastating earthquake three years later.

The amphitheatre riot is described by the historian Tacitus.[1] Breaking out during a gladiatorial show, it involved local supporters and visitors from Nuceria, and ended in a considerable number of deaths and injuries, especially among the

Nucerians. The full circumstances are unclear, but there may well have been a political dimension, because the matter was referred to the emperor, who asked the Roman Senate to adjudicate, and the consequent sanctions included the disbanding of what Tacitus describes mysteriously as 'illegal associations' as well as the exile of the games' organiser, who was himself a former senator. More seriously, the Pompeian amphitheatre was subjected to a 10-year closing order, depriving the city of its favourite entertainment. A well-known wall-painting from a house near the theatre quarter depicts the fateful fracas in graphic detail.

The earthquake struck on 5 February 62. Reference to the devastation appears again in the pages of Tacitus, but more especially in a treatise on natural phenomena written by Nero's tutor, the orator and man of letters L. Annaeus Seneca.[2] According to his account a large part of Pompeii was laid low, while Herculaneum and Nuceria too were affected, albeit less severely, and there was even some damage at Naples. The destruction at Pompeii was clearly extensive: many buildings collapsed or were seriously damaged, and very few did not require some degree of reconstruction and redecoration. Signs of emergency repairs, carried out in heterogeneous and salvaged materials, are to be seen everywhere. A favourite building technique of this phase – though not unfamiliar in the preceding period – was the so-called *opus vittatum mixtum*, or *listatum*, in which mortared rubble was faced with alternate courses of bricks and small blocks of stone (mainly Sarno stone, tuff or *cruma*). Particularly characteristic of the repair work, and generally executed either in *listatum* or in brickwork alone, are 'stitches' filling fissures which had developed within walls (*36*) or reinforcing the corners of buildings that had crumbled (*colour plate 14*). Epigraphic records of the reconstruction are scarce, but an inscription from the temple of Isis states that the building had collapsed in the earthquake and needed to be rebuilt 'from its foundations'. More vivid are a pair of quaint reliefs, one from a household shrine in the House of L. Caecilius Jucundus, the other of unknown provenance. Each shows the effects of the earthquake upon different monuments in the city (*37*).

It is clear that Pompeii never fully recovered from the effects of the disaster. The work of restoration, attested by the presence of piles of building stone and materials for making mortar and plaster, not to mention paint pots and half-finished wall-decorations, was still in progress in all parts of the city when the final catastrophe took place 17 years later. In house I.9.12, palynological analysis has revealed that some rooms were colonised by plants associated with damp conditions, indicating that roofs may not have been replaced.[3] Just as serious earthquakes of more recent times have necessitated decades of reconstruction, so the one that afflicted Pompeii left a prolonged legacy of ruin and disruption. To make matters worse, there were probably further earthquakes. In 64 we hear of one which affected Naples while Nero was giving a performance in the theatre (the building collapsed after he had left it).[4] In his account of the events of August 79, Pliny reports that the region was accustomed to frequent tremors

36 Brick stitch repairing a fissure caused by the earthquake of AD 62. *Photograph R.J. Ling 86 bis/34*

37 Cast of a relief depicting the earthquake of 62: House of L. Caecilius Jucundus (V.1.26). At the left, the collapse of the Capitolium and the adjacent arch (cf. *23*); at the right, a sacrifice. 13 x 86cm. *Photograph M. Thatcher (Ward-Perkins collection)*

and that there had been a number of them in the days preceding the eruption[5] – a circumstance which accords with what modern seismologists would expect in the lead-up to an explosive event of the Vesuvian type. It is possible, indeed, that some repairs in progress in 79 were caused not by the earthquake of 62 but by more recent shocks.

Yet we must beware of exaggerating the extent of the disruption. Many of Pompeii's wealthier householders, such as the Vettii brothers and the owner of the House of the Menander, were able to complete full-scale programmes of restoration, including luxurious wall-paintings, within their properties. The old idea that members of the ruling classes abandoned their town houses and retreated to their (putative) country estates does not square with the evidence.[6] Political life seems to have been conducted with the usual vigour, and the leading families continued to play their normal role in civic affairs. It appears, too, that the 10-year ban on gladiatorial games was rescinded, perhaps as a gesture of sympathy to the stricken city. And there is no reason to believe that any earthquakes in the years leading up to 79 entailed new damage on a scale comparable to that of 62: Pliny actually says of the pre-eruption tremors that they caused comparatively little alarm. Some of the repairs that were taking place at the time of the eruption, rather than implying recent damage, may have been 'secondary' interventions. Walls which had been re-erected quickly in the aftermath of the earthquake, to ensure that some sort of normal life could be maintained in a difficult situation, were being replaced by more carefully designed and durable structures. Alternatively, walls which had survived the event of 62 may have suffered insidious weakening which became apparent only after the passage of several years; in other words there could have been 'creeping' damage and delayed-action responses which explain why rebuilding was still in progress on the eve of the eruption.

A comparable situation may have occurred in relation to the city's water system. Excavations along the city's sidewalks, undertaken first by Amedeo Maiuri in 1931 and more recently by Salvatore Nappo in the 1990s, have revealed that this was non-functional in 79.[7] Isolated lengths of lead pipe were found, mainly on or close to the surface, but none of these extended for more than a few metres without interruption. Instead, there were trenches 60-90cm wide and up to 1.60m deep which had evidently been dug shortly before the eruption and were still open when the volcanic clinkers were falling (*38*). It seems unlikely that the water supply would have remained out of commission for 17 years when many city-dwellers were dependent on the street fountains: if pipes had been ruptured in the earthquake of 62, such damage would surely have been one of the first priorities in a reconstruction programme. What probably happened is that the water network was indeed restored in 62, with pipes laid along the surface (as they may have been, for convenience of repair, even before the earthquake), but this restoration was regarded as provisional and in 79 a new programme had been launched to install pipes at a deep level. Many of the necessary trenches had been dug, and the workmen involved had begun salvaging the existing pipes with a view to reusing them, but the operation was still unfinished when Vesuvius intervened.

A similar situation may be postulated in relation to public architecture. It has traditionally been argued that many of the city's public buildings were still in a state of ruin at the time of the eruption; only in houses and other projects involving private finance was the work of reconstruction well advanced. But independent studies by John Dobbins and Kurt Wallat have shown, for the buildings on the east side of the forum at least, that this view is misguided.[8] The appearance of devastation and incompleteness created, for example, by the disappearance of statues and the absence of marble wall-veneers should be credited to the activities of salvagers and plunderers after the city's burial. So, far from being incomplete, the buildings to the east of the forum seem to have been largely restored; moreover, their appearance was enhanced by the liberal use of marble veneers, and there was a deliberate effort to unify the façades by linking them and blocking the last vestiges of two east–west streets which formerly debouched in the forum. One edifice, the so-called Temple of the Public Lares,

38 Work on the water supply interrupted by the eruption of AD 79. In the foreground, filled with volcanic lapilli, is a trench which had just been dug; in the background are a pair of water pipes running along the surface of the sidewalk (south side of *insula* VII.2). *Photograph S.C. Nappo*

may have been constructed *ex novo*: the way in which it uses a play of curved and rectangular recesses to model interior space recalls certain elements in Nero's Golden House in Rome and, from our knowledge of Roman architecture, would have been unusually avant garde before this time.

A difference of the post-earthquake period lay in the source of funding. To restore their major public buildings after the earthquake the Pompeians must have had at least some financial support from the central government. The civil wars which followed the death of Nero ended in December 69 with the accession of Vespasian, who inaugurated a new era of administrative efficiency in which one of the main propaganda planks was the emperor's concern for the welfare of the people, including those afflicted by disasters. The plight of the earthquake-affected region in Campania could not have escaped his notice. For the recovery programme the traditional pattern of reliance upon private munificence was clearly impracticable: the extent of the work required would have placed an unreasonable burden on the local magistrates. Presumably, therefore, help was provided by the emperor, as it had been in the case of earlier natural disasters, such as the earthquake which had struck various cities of Asia Minor in AD 17. At Herculaneum there is specific evidence of imperial intervention in the form of a couple of inscriptions dating to 76, one of which states that Vespasian restored the temple of the Mother of the Gods (the Magna Mater), which had 'collapsed in the earthquake', while the other, though woefully incomplete, has been interpreted as commemorating a similar gesture in relation to a statue of the Genius Municipi Herculanei (the Spirit of the City of Herculaneum).[9] No such document survives at Pompeii; but evidence of the emperor's interest in the city is provided by a text recorded on slabs found outside the Herculaneum, Vesuvius, Nuceria and Marine Gates (*39*). This reveals that Vespasian sent a special commissioner, T. Suedius Clemens, to reclaim for the community public land which had been illegally occupied by private individuals – evidently land which fell within the *pomerium*, the 100ft wide swathe which ran along the exterior of the old city walls.[10] If the emperor played an active part in asserting public property rights at Pompeii, it is highly probable that he also contributed to the work of post-earthquake regeneration.

In addition to the buildings of the forum, a priority in the programme of reconstruction would have been the sanctuary of Venus. This is usually said still to have resembled a builder's yard in AD 79, but again the state of incompleteness could be partially due to post-eruption stone-robbing. Here, however, a further factor may have been the radical nature of the rebuilding: the old sanctuary was being replaced by a new and grander project. That the temple precinct was enlarged after the middle of the first century AD is shown by the fact that new foundations were cut through rooms of the so-called Imperial Villa which were painted in the Fourth Style. The most likely date for this development, since it presupposes the abandonment of the Imperial Villa, would be after the earthquake: it is even possible that the villa, which projected into the *pomerium*,

39 Inscription, outside the Nuceria Gate, recording the commission of T. Suedius Clemens to reclaim public land illegally occupied in the zone outside the city walls. Between AD 69 and 79. *Photograph J.B. Ward-Perkins*

was one of the properties expropriated by Suedius Clemens. In all probability, therefore, the temple of Venus offers another illustration of the vigour with which the programme of recovery was being pursued at the time of the eruption.

One last modification to the public landscape of Pompeii is securely placed after the earthquake: the building of the Central Baths. Situated like the other intramural baths at a major crossroads, the intersection of Via Stabiana and Via di Nola, these were evidently necessitated by increasing pressure upon the Forum and Stabian Baths. At the same time, they introduced modern developments in the architecture of thermal establishments such as had become established in the great imperial baths of the capital. Aided by technical improvements in wall-heating and in the production of window-glass, the designers of the new baths were able to dispense with the old dark, inward-looking architecture and replace it with spacious rooms lit by large south-west facing windows. The site for the new baths was obtained by taking over a whole block and demolishing the pre-existing houses, presumably after expropriation. Such a drastic re-development may have been more easily undertaken in the aftermath of the earthquake, which had left properties damaged or deserted; nonetheless it shows that Pompeii was no moribund city simply struggling to recover from the disaster of 62. It was alive and receptive to new urban forms. Had it survived, Pompeii would have continued to evolve in sympathy with the changing requirements of new generations just as it had done in the past.

The last years of Pompeii were also a golden age for wall-painting. The Fourth Style (*colour plate 15*), which was evolving by the reign of Claudius (AD 41-54), was the most fantastic and playful form of painted decoration devised in antiquity. In broad terms it represented a revival of the architectural illusionism of the Second Style but instead of the solid, believable structures of the earlier period painters retained the spindly proportions and fairytale forms of the Third Style, now rendered in warm golden colours and stacked up in breathtaking visions of infinite space and recession. Central pictures continued to be a feature, though the panels were relatively small and square (*colour plate 16*), and tended to appear as if hung upon great coloured tapestries (for which yellow and red were the preferred colours) rather than framed by pavilions. A favourite scheme offered a rhythmic alternation of these picture-bearing 'tapestries' and visual openings containing perspectival architecture upon a white ground. Alternatively, the entire wall was opened to create a framework of architecture in which groups of figures played out scenes from well-known myths, like actors in a baroque stage-set.

The finest of these decorations show no decline in standards from the work of earlier periods. Even in the aftermath of the earthquake the quality of many new paintings, such as those in the House of the Vettii, was exceptional: where householders had the resources to hire accomplished craftsmen and pay for the best materials, they did not hesitate to do so. Naturally there were houses whose repairs and redecorations were less careful, and some where they were downright crude, but the lavish attention bestowed on the repainting of the grand mansions confirms that the city elite was still prepared to invest in its properties. This situation continued to apply right to the end. A team of painters was working on a particularly ornate reception room in a house in IX.12 at the very moment when the eruption began; they fled, leaving frescoes half-finished and abandoning their paint-pots and other equipment.[11] There is no more vivid illustration of how the activity of artistic production – and the business of life in general – was cut off abruptly while in full flow.

1 *Above* Painting of Venus in a shell. Rear wall of the garden in the House of the Marine Venus (II.3.3). *Photograph D. Trillo*

2 *Right* Interior of the Basilica. Late second century BC. *Photograph D. Trillo*

3 Opposite above First Style wall-decoration in the House of Sallust (VI.2.4). Second or early first century BC. *Photograph E. de Maré*

4 Opposite below Alexander the Great in battle. Detail of a mosaic pavement from the House of the Faun (VI.12.2). Late second or early first century BC. Naples Museum 10020. *Photograph Getty Research Library, Wim Swaan collection 96.P.21*

5 Above Opus quasi reticulatum with triangular brick quoins. Detail of the small theatre, built soon after 80 BC. *Photograph Ward-Perkins collection*

6 Right Second Style wall-painting in the Villa of the Mysteries. Second quarter of first century BC. *Photograph E. de Maré*

7 *Opposite above* Reticulate wall with coloured patterns: façade of VIII.2.30. *Photograph L.A. Ling*

8 *Opposite below* Interior of the Large Palaestra. Augustan period (turn of the first centuries BC and AD). *Photograph D. Trillo*

9 *Right* Limestone colonnade in the forum. First half of first century AD. *Photograph D. Trillo*

10 *Below* Painting of a *paradeisos* (safari park) in the garden of the House of the Ceii (I.6.15). Between AD 62 and 79. *Photograph D. Trillo*

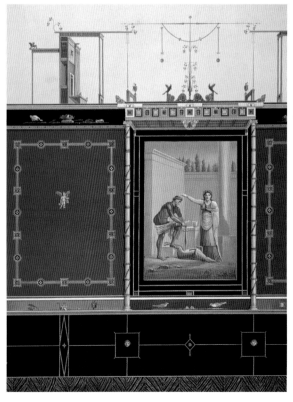

11 *Above* Tomb of Vestorius Priscus (between AD 62 and 79): painting of silver plate on the inner face of the enclosure wall. *Photograph L.A. Ling and R.J. Ling*

12 *Left* Third Style wall-painting in the House of M. Spurius Mesor (VII.3.29). First quarter of first century AD. *Colour lithograph in A. Mau,* Geschichte der decorativen Wandmalerei in Pompeji *(1882)*

13 *Right* Painting of Pan and the nymphs, from the House of Jason (IX.5.18). Third Style (first quarter of first century AD). 1.20 x 0.93m. Naples Museum 111473. *Photograph Ward-Perkins collection*

14 *Below* Post-earthquake repair in brickwork: south-west corner of the Building of Eumachia. *Photograph J.B. Ward-Perkins*

15 Fourth Style wall-paintings. House of the
Vestals (VI.1.7). Third quarter of first century
AD. 2.30 x 2.00m. Naples Museum 9701.
Photograph Ward-Perkins collection

16 Theseus after the killing of the
Minotaur, from the House of M. Gavius
Rufus (VII.2.16). Fourth Style (third
quarter of first century AD). 97 x 98cm.
Naples Museum 9043. *Photograph Ward-
Perkins collection*

17 *Right* Bronze statue of Apollo in the temple of Apollo. *Photograph D. Trillo*

18 *Below* Gold lamp found in the area of the temple of Venus. Ht 15.1cm, length 23.3cm. Naples Museum 25000. *Photograph Ward-Perkins collection*

19 Wall plaque with a relief of a phallus on legs. Nuceria tuff in a terracotta frame. 31.5 x 36.5cm. Pompeii III.4, south-east corner. *Photograph D. Trillo*

20 Examples of *terra sigillata* pottery, including decorated bowls made in Italy (top) and southern Gaul (left). *Photograph S.A. Hay and A. Sibthorpe*

21 Painting of Bacchus and Mount Vesuvius from the House of the Centenary (IX.8.6). The god, enveloped in grapes, symbolises the importance of viticulture in the area; the volcano has its pre-79 configuration, conical and covered with vegetation. 1.40 x 1.01m. Naples Museum 112286. *Photograph University of Bologna*

22 Bakery at VII.2.22. At the right are mills for grinding grain, at the left an oven for baking the bread. *Photograph D. Trillo*

23 Large Theatre, viewed from the south-west. *Photograph D. Trillo*

24 *Right* Painted portrait
of Menander. House of the
Menander (I.10.4). Between AD
62 and 79. Ht 1.08m. *Photograph
E. de Maré*

25 *Below* Terracotta figurines of
gladiators from Pompeii. Ht 13
and 14cm. Naples Museum 20259,
20341. *Photograph Ward-Perkins
collection*

28 *Opposite above* Blue glass stemmed goblet. Ht 14cm, diameter at rim 15.5cm. Naples Museum 76/215. *Photograph Ward-Perkins collection*

29 *Opposite below* Silver cup decorated with reliefs: the Labours of Heracles. From the House of the Menander (I.10.4). Ht 8cm, diameter at rim 11.5cm. Naples Museum 145506. *Photograph Ward-Perkins collection*

26 Bronze gladiator's helmet from the quadriportico next to the theatre. Ht 45.5cm. Naples Museum 5650. *Photograph Ward-Perkins collection*

27 Satyr mask: detail of reliefs on one of a pair of bronze gladiators' greaves from the quadriportico next to the theatre. Naples Museum 5666-7. *Photograph Ward-Perkins collection*

30 Ivory dice, knucklebones and bone gaming pieces. Diameter of counters from 3 to 3.5cm. Naples Museum. *Photograph Ward-Perkins collection*

31 Colour lithograph of Third Style paintings in the House of the Bronzes or Black Wall (VII.4.59). First quarter of first century AD. *After W. Zahn,* Die schönsten Ornamente und merkwürdigsten Gemälde aus Pompeji, Herculaneum und Stabiae *(1828-59)*

6

LIFE IN THE CITY

The previous chapters have sought to reconstruct the history of Pompeii up
to the eruption. We can now undertake a general review of life in the city in
its final years. As a result of the circumstances of its burial, and the nature of past
excavations, which have concentrated overwhelmingly upon simply uncovering
the 'time capsule' of AD 79, Pompeii acquires especial importance as a source of
information on society and economics in a small Italian community of the third
quarter of the first century AD.

DEMOGRAPHY

How many people lived in the city at the time of the eruption?[1] This is a question
which has often been asked, but to which no conclusive answer has been given.
Estimates have ranged from little more than 6,000 to well over 20,000. The
basis for any calculation is, of course, primarily the walled area, and the crudest
method is merely to extrapolate from a hypothetical figure of population per
hectare. On this basis Beloch in 1898 arrived at a total of 15,000, while Russell
in 1977, using comparative data from medieval cities, got a figure of 6,400-6,700.
But such methods run up against the difficulty that the distribution of residential
buildings is far from regular – large areas in the south-west quarter are taken up
by public buildings or open piazzas – and that we cannot be sure what lies in
the unexcavated two fifths of the city. The 1950s excavations in Regions I and II
revealed a much sparser pattern of building, with large parts of *insulae* occupied
by vineyards, market gardens and the like, than could have been anticipated from
the previously excavated districts. Population density clearly varied from one
zone to another.

A more scientific approach is to estimate the number of dwelling units in the city and assign a hypothetical number of inhabitants to each. But this method too has produced wildly varying results. Fiorelli made a rough count of the number of houses and shops in the portion of the city excavated in 1872 and extrapolated from there to get an overall total of 1,800. Nissen a few years later, arguing that Fiorelli had underestimated the number of rooms on ground floors and taken insufficient account of upstairs apartments, somewhat arbitrarily doubled the figure to 3,600. But the sparser housing revealed by the excavations in the east of the city counsels a reduction. Recent estimates by Andrew Wallace-Hadrill (1991), based on our current knowledge of the city, have produced a total of only 1,200 or 1,300.

But even knowing the number of houses does not get us much nearer an informed estimate of the population. Dwellings can range from one- or two-room units to mansions covering more than 2000sq m, and there is no certainty as to how densely each establishment was occupied. Fiorelli roughly calculated the number of rooms in his sample and from this achieved a total of 12,000 people. Nissen, having made a generous allowance for upstairs accommodation, reached a total of 20,000. This higher figure gained general acceptance during the first half of the twentieth century. It seemed to acquire additional authority from the estimated capacity of the amphitheatre, which was also put at 20,000. But, even if the estimate for the amphitheatre is right (it too is a crude figure, based on a hypothetical amount of seating space assigned to each spectator), we cannot assume comparability with the size of the city's population: the episode of the riot of AD 59 shows clearly that performances were attended not only by the local population but also by visitors from neighbouring cities. Recent population estimates, taking into account the new data from the 1950s excavations, have tended to be much lower. A new survey by Eschebach in 1970 reduced the total to 8,000, and figures between 8,000 and 10,000 have now become widely accepted.

There is still no satisfactory way of fine-tuning the arithmetic. Eschebach did not count numbers of rooms, but merely calculated the proportion of the city which was occupied by houses (approximately 40 hectares) and applied a notional figure of 200 inhabitants per hectare. If we wished to achieve greater precision, a more refined technique might be to work out how much sleeping accommodation was available. But attempts to identify bedrooms, using the recorded remains of beds or the evidence of architectural features, especially alcoves or shallow recesses marking the former presence of beds, are of limited efficacy, since many potential bedrooms on upper floors are destroyed or only imperfectly known, while even on ground floors there will have been many bedrooms that lacked recesses and many wooden beds that have left no trace; moreover, many household members, such as slaves, certainly slept on mattresses on the floor. The situation is rendered more complex by the exceptional conditions pertaining in the city's last years. The effects of the devastating earthquake of 62 and possible further earthquakes shortly before 79 must have had a demographic impact. Even if householders did not leave the city in large numbers, as once believed, there may well have been some houses that were closed up or abandoned, and there was almost certainly an influx of builders and craftsmen involved in the reconstruction programme. The population statistics of AD 79 may have been anything but normal.

In the end, we can make only rough estimates. Accepting that the old figure of 20,000, which would entail an average density of 315 inhabitants per hectare (127 per acre), without any allowance for public buildings and other uninhabited spaces, is much too high, we should probably work on the basis that the currently fashionable figure of 8,000–10,000 is nearer the mark. This, of course, makes no allowance for Pompeii's *territorium*. Working on the basis that this extended south as far as the crossing of the River Sarno, north to the slopes of Vesuvius, west as far as the limits of the *territorium* of Herculaneum, and east roughly halfway to Nuceria, we can estimate the available area as about 130sq km. Using Beloch's estimate for average population density in Campania of 180 persons per sq km (including urban areas), this would produce an overall total of some 23,000, of whom more than half lived outside the city walls. Such a ratio of extramural to intramural population need not cause surprise. The sporadic excavations which have taken place to the south and south-west of the city indicate intensive development of the riverside and port areas, and there seems to have been a thick sprinkling of *villae rusticae*, not to mention more luxurious villas, throughout the countryside round the north and east of the city. Although the figures are highly conjectural, they provide a plausible working model.

How large a proportion of the population died in the eruption, we shall probably never know. There have been various guesses as to the number of victims, with Fiorelli's figure of 2,000 gaining widespread acceptance. But any exact computation is complicated by the fact that, for the first century or more of the excavations, there was little interest in recording, still less recovering, human remains. Nor can we be sure that the victims found in the excavated parts of the city can be regarded as a representative sample: the finding in the 1970s of a group of fugitives outside the Nola Gate (together with the younger Pliny's account of his own experience at Misenum) suggests that many people may have fled into the countryside before they were overtaken by the fatal surges. It is also possible that considerable numbers of people had fled to the coast, as did the elder Pliny and his friends, in the hope of being rescued by sea. It used to be thought that the bulk of the population of Herculaneum had escaped before the 1980s excavations revealed that hundreds of victims had taken shelter in vaulted chambers on the ancient sea-front. Something similar may have happened at Pompeii.

An attempt in 1996 to count the skeletons recorded in the excavation diaries has at least produced firmer statistics for the excavated zones.[2] Dividing these individuals into those found in the initial layers of pumice (up to a height of 2.60–

2.80m), who may have been trapped or killed by collapsing masonry or the like, and those found at a higher level, in the strata of ash deposited by the pyroclastic surges, we have totals respectively of 394 bodies (200 of which occurred singly and 194 in groups) and 650 bodies (152 singletons and 498 in groups). The total of 1,044 individuals should be supplemented by generic references to groups of skeletons or simply to the finding of bones, and an overall estimate produces a grand total of 1,150. Even this cannot be a final figure, given that many skeletons were either not noticed or not recorded; but it represents a more accurate census than any carried out before. It also allows some conclusions to be drawn about how people died. Whereas most of the victims of the early phase were found in the interior of houses, a high percentage of those who died in the pyroclastic surges were in the streets or open spaces, and most of these were evidently heading for the country to the south and east. By this stage, 18 or 20 hours after the eruption had begun, they had decided that there was no future in waiting for the situation to improve.

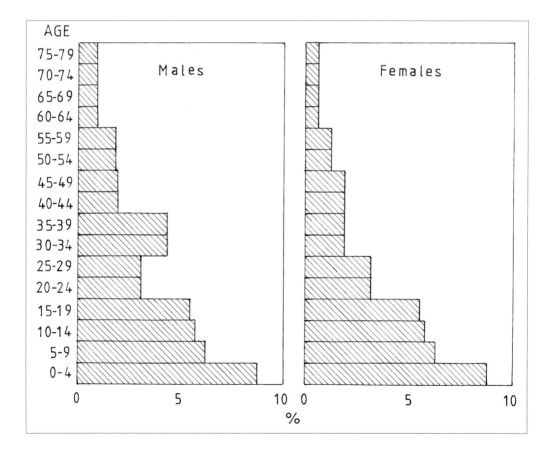

40 Age profile of victims of the eruption. *Drawing R.J. Ling, after M. and R.J. Henneberg in* Homo Faber: natura, scienza e tecnica nell'antica Pompei *(1999)*

Only in the last 25 years has there been any systematic effort to undertake scientific study of the skeletons.[3] Given that these are the remains of people who did not die from disease or natural causes, they provide a good opportunity to establish patterns of age and sex, and of possible pathological problems, within a cross-section of the population of an urban community of this period. Projections from the available data (*40*) suggest that the sex ratio of those who died was roughly 1:1 and that their average age was about 25, with a median around 40 (for males 41, females 39). At the higher end of the age-range there was a fair-sized proportion of people over 60, but about half the population is likely to have consisted (as normal in ancient societies) of children or adolescents. The fact that child skeletons are under-represented in the Pompeian collections may be due to the neglect of early excavators rather than to any real dearth of them: that only 81 of the 1,044 bodies recorded in the excavation diaries are specified as those of infants, can scarcely conform to reality. At the same time, the statistics reveal fewer young men than might have been expected in a random sample, which reinforces the idea that many of the most able-bodied had fled the city in the early stages of the disaster.

Further results of skeletal analysis have been in the fields of morphology, ethnology and pathology. It has proved possible, for instance, to estimate average heights for adult males and females – 1.66m for men, 1.53m for women – and to determine, from DNA analysis, the racial make-up of the population. While the majority of people were, as one would expect, of European stock, there was some evidence for the possible presence of individuals from Africa. In terms of pathology, there is evidence of the occurrence of arthritis, tooth decay, injuries (including healed bone fractures), and rarer conditions such as Paget's disease; in addition, 11 per cent of adult Pompeians appear to have suffered from *spina bifida*. It is likely that continuing studies of skeletal material will add more detail in all these areas.

CIVIC ADMINISTRATION

The city of Pompeii in 79 was, naturally, subject to the authority of the Roman state, and all citizens of Pompeii were also citizens of Rome; but, like every other city in the Empire, it had its own local government. For information on how this functioned we are dependent upon inscriptions and upon analogies with the constitutions of other Roman cities. The chief executive officers, like the consuls of Rome, were appointed in pairs, following the traditional belief in dualism as a safeguard against possible abuses of power. Again like Rome's consuls, these officers held power only for a year (from 1 July to 30 June) and could not be re-elected until some years, normally five, had elapsed. The senior pair of officers were the duovirs, who presided over meetings of the city council and, as their full title (*duumviri iure dicundo*) indicates, administered justice in local assizes. Junior to them, and an essential stepping stone on the career path to the duovirate, were a pair of aediles, responsible for the maintenance of streets, the supervision of markets, and policing. These four officials supervised all the day-to-day business of civic administration, but every five years the duovirs were designated *quinquennales* and had the special duty of conducting a census. The position of *quinquennalis*, for which only those with previous experience of holding the duovirate were normally eligible, represented the pinnacle of a career in local government.

These officials, like their counterparts in Rome, received no formal remuneration for their services. It was regarded as an honour to serve the city, and holders of office were expected not only to pay their own expenses, including the costs of employing staff (scribes and other assistants), but to dig deep into their pockets to provide benefits for their fellow citizens. Among these benefits were the shows in the amphitheatre, distributions of food and gifts to the people, and − at the top end of the scale − public buildings. As noted in earlier chapters, many public buildings were constructed, or refurbished, by duovirs who advertised their generosity in dedicatory inscriptions, declaring that the work had been funded from their own resources (*41*). As a result, the local leaders inevitably came from an elite of the wealthiest citizens: only they could sustain the burdens of office.

41 Inscription from the Stabian Baths recording the addition of a *laconicum* (hot dry room) and *destrictarium* (rubbing-down room) and alterations to the porticoes and *palaestra* (exercise court). The duumvirs P. Uulius and P. Aninius financed the work 'from the money which they were legally obliged to spend on games and monuments'. Soon after 80 BC? Naples Museum 3826. *Photograph Ward-Perkins collection*

There was, of course, a local treasury, and many public works were funded from this. The fact that officers vaunted their personal munificence implies that other buildings and services were paid for by the city. There must also have been city employees, though whether they were engaged on a long-term salaried basis is questionable, and some of them may have been slaves. The city also had funds to reward distinguished citizens. The epitaphs of duovirs and aediles record subsidies towards the cost of their funerals granted by the local council. How this money was raised, we do not know. It is possible that some of it came from personal contributions made by councillors. There must also have been income from the renting of property and from forms of local taxation. In a city which controlled a river port and road communications at the hub of a fertile region, an important factor is likely to have been a port tax or customs dues. By one means or another sufficient funds would have been generated.

Alongside the executive officers there was a deliberative body, the local council, which consisted of 80-100 leading citizens, the *decuriones*, recruited predominantly from those who had held public office (anyone who had attained the post of aedile automatically became a councillor for life). The role of the council, like the senate in Rome or a modern parliament, was to debate general issues of policy and to exercise control over the magistrates, who were technically bound by its decisions. Given the powers of this body, it was important to ensure that its quality was maintained. Councillors must be of free birth and of good character, and must satisfy a minimum property qualification. It was one of the jobs of the *quinquennales* to weed out any councillors who had, for financial, moral or other reasons, become unworthy of office, and to appoint new members in their place. A steady infusion of new blood would, in theory, ensure that the council's debates remained vigorous and that there would never be a shortage of candidates for the executive posts.

That these posts – for all the costs of holding office – were avidly sought after, is revealed by the evidence of election campaigning.[4] The annual elections were where the people – or at least that element of the people that was enfranchised, namely males of free birth or status – had their say. And, to ensure that they exercised their voting rights, the walls of all the main streets, and many minor ones too, were turned into billboards for election posters.

The election posters, actually notices painted directly on the plaster or on a layer of whitewash, are the most striking legacy of political life in the city. Their format is fairly standard. The names of a candidate or candidates, in large letters, are followed first by the office for which he or they are standing, then by the formula 'O.V.F.' (*oro vos faciatis*: 'I ask you to vote for'); in a number of cases we are also given the name of the person who is doing the canvassing, accompanied by the verb *rogat* ('asks [for your support]'). Sometimes the notice concludes with the name of the sign-painter, usually a professional calligrapher operating with assistants (though sometimes a non-specialist who boasted of working unaided). The information contained in the notices can tell us much about patterns of political rivalry and electoral support. There were no political parties in the modern sense, but certain candidates clearly formed alliances, with pairs of candidates running together for the duovirate or for the aedileship, and even slates of four candidates running together for the four posts. The candidates, many of whom belonged to families which remained prominent in civic life from generation to generation, sometimes appear to have enjoyed concentrations of support in particular neighbourhoods, possibly the neighbourhoods in which they lived; but just as often their support was not confined to any one area – something which improved their chances of success, since the election results were based on the number of constituencies won, not the overall count of votes. The canvassers, on the other hand, tended to put up notices only in the area of their own houses.

The canvassers were not solely individuals, but also include *vicini* (neighbours, or generally members of the same ward) and special-interest groups such as particular kinds of craftsmen. All this might, on the face of it, suggest a flourishing democratic process, but it is questionable how far the man in the street was truly interested in politics. Similarities in wording between posters in support of given candidates, even where the sponsors were nominally different, imply that campaigns were centrally organised, much as in today's elections. And many voters will have felt constrained by networks of patronage and personal obligation. In other words, the posters were designed primarily to remind Pompeians of their civic duty, and they tell us more about the energy of the candidates and their supporters than about the enthusiasm of the electorate at large.

One factor that would have guaranteed a steady supply of candidates was the aspirations of the upwardly mobile classes – self-made traders, manufacturers, or financiers, some of them from freedman stock, who wanted to register their 'arrival' in Pompeian society by holding civic office. A possible case in point is A. Umbricius Scaurus, who held the duovirate towards the middle of the first century AD: either he or, more probably, his father (who survived him and built his tomb) managed a large business for the production of fish sauce, and it may have been this that provided him with the wherewithal to pursue a political career.[5] Much clearer is the example of N. Popidius Ampliatus, who restored the Temple of Isis, damaged by the earthquake of AD 62, in the name of his six-year-old son N. Popidius Celsinus; in reward for this act of munificence, the city councillors admitted the son to their number, thus opening the way for him to hold the public offices to which his father, probably a freedman, was denied access.[6]

For election purposes the citizens were apparently divided into five voting groups, depending on where they lived. The names of these groups are known from election programmes in which they occur. The Forenses evidently lived in the south-west quarter, in the vicinity of the forum; the Urbulanenses in the south-east and east central quarter, in proximity to the Porta Urbulana (what

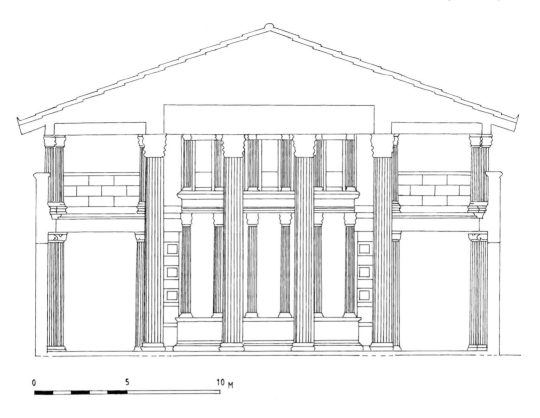

42 Section of the Basilica, facing west. Late second century BC. *Drawing L.A. Ling, after K.F. Ohr, Das Basilika in Pompeji (1991)*

we today call the Sarno Gate); the Salinienses in the area of the Porta Salis or Saliniensis, the ancient name of the Herculaneum Gate; and the Campanenses in the north-east quarter, in the area of the Porta Campana, which was probably the ancient name of today's Nola Gate. Finally, the Pagani were those who lived in the surrounding *territorium*, the Pagus Augustus Felix Suburbanus.

The city's administrative buildings, as noted in Chapter 1, were clustered round the south end of the forum (4). The largest and grandest was the Basilica, at the south-west corner. This was an early example of a type of aisled building which opened onto the forum in many Roman cities, serving as a palace of justice and a hall for various kinds of public meetings. In the Pompeian version, unlike many similar buildings in other cities, the main entrance was at the narrow end, with an unroofed vestibule and a set of four steps leading up to a columnar screen which framed the openings to the interior. Internally (*42, colour plate 2*), the space was divided into a nave and aisles by two rows of monumental columns, which also turned across to leave a passage at each end; the side walls were articulated by small semi-columns in two tiers, each corresponding to one of the free-standing columns; and lighting was provided by windows in the spaces between the semi-columns in the upper storey. At the rear was a two-storeyed tribunal from which the duovirs could dispense justice or address audiences. That the building was frequently thronged by people is indicated by the number and variety of messages carved in the plaster of the walls, including one naming the consuls of 78 BC which gives a *terminus ante quem* for the date of construction. So numerous were the graffiti that one wit, repeating a message scrawled in other public places, expressed wonderment that the wall had not collapsed under the weight of them.[7]

At the south end of the forum are three similarly sized halls which almost certainly had administrative functions, but over whose specific roles there is no agreement. All are extensively rebuilt in brick-faced concrete, indicating that, in their final form at least, they belong to the Imperial period; however, all three have yielded evidence of earlier phases in which their façades were set further back and on different alignments, which suggests that they were not originally part of a unitary programme. They have usually been identified respectively, from east to west, as a hall in which the aediles conducted their business, a senate chamber, and a hall for the duovirs. The apsidal treatment of the rear wall in each of the outer chambers would certainly be consonant with places where audiences were held, with the presiding officers seated in state in the apse; but the central hall, whose walls are punctuated by regular series of niches suitable to contain shelving, may better be interpreted as a *tabularium*, where the city's archives were stored. Perhaps one of the outer chambers was where magistrates conducted small audiences and committee meetings, as opposed to the major public meetings held in the Basilica, while the other was the meeting place of the council.

The final administrative structure faced the Basilica from the east side of the forum. Rather than a building in the conventional sense, this was an open enclosure, squarish in shape, originally accessible from the forum and from Via dell'Abbondanza to the north by a series of openings (five on the west and four on the north) between pillars. Access from the street could be regulated by the erection of a temporary barrier, the holes for whose stanchions are preserved along the outer edge of the sidewalk. It has been plausibly argued that this structure was the Comitium, or voting enclosure, where municipal elections were held. A tribunal set in a recess at the middle of the south wall may have been used by the presiding officer, one of the outgoing duovirs. At the time of the eruption, all but two of the western entrances and one of the northern ones had been closed, perhaps because of structural weaknesses triggered by earthquake damage.

RELIGION

Religion in Pompeii, as in all ancient societies, encompassed a multiplicity of deities with different characters and different spheres of competence, and people could cultivate now one, now another, depending upon their personal preferences or upon the needs of the moment.

Evidence for religious belief and practice comes primarily from the remains of temples and altars. At the top of the scale were the grand public temples of 'official' deities, mostly set in monumental precincts; below these were slightly more modest temples associated with other Greco-Roman and imported gods, as well as the newly emerging cults associated with the imperial house; and at the bottom of the scale were small streetside shrines, or indeed shrines within the home, dedicated to various deities, but all designed for personal prayers and offerings.

Of the official deities the longest established were those of the temple in the Triangular Forum and the precinct on the west side of the main forum. The former temple was set on a low stepped platform and enclosed on all sides by a colonnade (peristyle) characteristic of Greek temples; the presence of Doric capitals with a broad saucer-shaped profile enable the original structure to be dated to the second half of the sixth century BC.[8] The numbers of columns in the peristyle, according to the most likely restoration seven at front and back and 11 along the sides, does not conform to normal Greek patterns, where 6 x 13 became the rule; but a possible explanation is suggested by the discovery of an off-centre statue base within the temple's inner chamber (*cella*). Rather than a single cult statue, best seen through the central intercolumniation of a six-column façade, there may have been a pair of statues side by side, which would have demanded an odd number of façade columns. Which deities were represented by the statues is uncertain; but one of them is likely to have been Minerva (Athena), whose temple is named in the nearest of the *eítuns* inscriptions, found on Via dell'Abbondanza to the north. A sculptured metope from the temple (*13*) depicts the myth of Ixion, punished by being tied to a wheel, with Athena and Hephaestus in attendance; and it is possible that ownership of our temple, like the Hephaesteum (so-called Theseum) in Athens, was shared by these two craft deities. But terracotta antefixes (roof-edge tiles) from a restoration of the second century BC represent Minerva and her protégé Heracles, suggesting a different conjunction. Heracles, the legendary hero who accomplished superhuman tasks, as well as founding neighbouring Herculaneum, was a favourite in domestic cults at Pompeii, as in the rest of the Roman world.

The precinct to the west of the forum had a history going back to the sixth century BC: excavations have revealed imported Athenian and Corinthian black-figure pottery of this time (see Chapter 2). But in its final form – a monumental temple set axially within a court surrounded by two-storeyed colonnades (the lower Ionic and the upper Corinthian) – it belongs to a much later period.

The temple itself is of Italian type, raised on a high podium with access via a monumental stairway at the front; round it ran a peristyle of Corinthian columns, six at the front and back and nine at the sides. The pavement of the *cella* contained a fine example of the pattern of rhomboidal pieces of green, white and grey stone arranged to produce an effect of cubes in perspective which fascinated patrons of the late second and early first centuries BC; and in the border was set a dedicatory inscription naming an official of the Samnite period.[9] From this evidence it would appear that the modernisation of the sanctuary took place before 89; but, if so, there were further important changes in later periods. A new altar was inaugurated in the early years of the Roman colony, and the construction of a western precinct wall in Augustan times implies a major rebuilding (see Chapter 4). Finally, the entrances from the forum on the east, originally a regular series of openings separated by pillars, were all blocked, apart from three opposite the side of the temple. That the deity of this temple was Apollo is established by a reference to that god in the pavement inscription and by the presence in the temple *cella* of an egg-shaped block of tuff which evidently represented Apollo's sacred 'navel stone' (the *omphalos*) at Delphi. Bronze statues of Apollo (*colour plate 17*) and his sister Diana (Artemis) stood in the precinct.

Two other monumental temples belonging to 'official' gods are those of Jupiter and Venus. The temple of Jupiter, at the north end of the forum (*23*), may have been built in the second half of the second century BC, but it was adapted in 80 BC by the Roman colonists to become a Capitolium, that is a temple of the Capitoline Triad, Jupiter, Juno and Minerva, such as was established in every colony of the conquered territories. This phase was marked by a rebuilding with a deep entrance porch framed by a screen of columns on three sides (six at the front and four on each flank) and an equally deep *cella* containing two-storeyed colonnades along the internal side walls. In the rear of this *cella* was a broad base designed to carry statues of the three deities. A wall-decoration of the early Second Style confirms the Sullan dating. The whole edifice was elevated on a high podium approached by a stairway whose lower part embraced a platform on which stood the temple's altar, suitably elevated for ceremonies to be performed in clear view of crowds in the forum.

The sanctuary of Venus, on a terrace at the south-west corner of the old city, resembled that of Apollo in having an axial temple building within a colonnaded court. It is generally accepted that construction took place in 80 BC or soon after, when Sulla's protecting goddess Venus Felix was adopted as patron of the new colony under the name Venus Pompeiana. The cult statue of the temple, now lost, may be reflected in an image known from various paintings at Pompeii which show the goddess heavily draped and wearing the mural crown of a city personification, with a ship's rudder – a clear reference to Pompeii's connections with maritime trade – supporting her left hand and a figure of Cupid standing on a pedestal next to her. The finding of votive offerings in the form of a bronze rudder and a marble statuette of Venus taking a bath guarantee that the deity of the temple has been correctly identified. As in many other Greek and Italian sanctuaries of the late second and first centuries BC, the porticoes may have been restricted to three sides only, leaving an open view over the valley; but the collapse of the substructures on this side precludes a clear understanding of what happened. As already noted, an ambitious reconstruction may have been underway after the earthquake of 62. The temple may, indeed, have been an early beneficiary of imperial interest. A spectacular discovery from the area of the sanctuary, a large gold lamp (*colour plate 18*), has been linked with evidence of a possible visit and donation by Nero in 64.[10]

Of the other traditional Greco-Roman gods the only one represented within the city walls was the healing god Aesculapius – accepting that the recent reinterpretation of the so-called Temple of Jupiter Meilichius is correct.[11] This small shrine in a constricted plot amid houses north of the theatre may go back to the late third or second century BC but seems to have been rebuilt in the quasi-reticulate technique of the Sullan period. It yielded terracotta statues of Aesculapius and Salus (Health), together with a bust of Minerva which was perhaps a later addition. Otherwise, we know of at least two temples outside the urban area. The sea god Neptune apparently received worship in the area of the port, while a sanctuary of Bacchus (Dionysus) has been excavated to the south-east of the city. The latter, built around the turn of the third and second centuries BC, featured a sculptured pediment with reclining figures of Dionysus and Aphrodite.

Alongside the old Greco-Roman deities a relative newcomer was the Egyptian goddess Isis, whose cult spread across the Mediterranean during the third and second centuries BC after the Greek conquest of Egypt. Giver of life, protector of the family, a goddess of healing and deliverance, she tended to absorb other deities and came close to being a universal goddess. Her control over destiny and the demands that she placed upon the worshipper made her cult particularly attractive as a personal religion, and she enjoyed favour not only among the well-to-do classes but also among ordinary people, including women and slaves. Her temple in Pompeii (*43*) probably dates to Augustan or early Julio-Claudian times,[12] but, as the inscription of N. Popidius Celsinus demonstrates, it was restored after the earthquake of 62. Situated in an enclosure above the theatre, it consisted not only of the temple proper, constructed on a high podium with a frontal stairway, but also of a little purificatory shrine (*purgatorium*) where worshippers were cleansed with sacred water from the Nile. At the rear of the precinct was the *ekklesiasterion*, a large room which may have served for the performance of sacred plays depicting the myth of the goddess and her consort Osiris. The whole complex was embellished with paintings and stucco reliefs of Egyptian subjects, including representations of Isiac priests and cult objects such as the little bucket (*situla*) for sacred milk and the rattle (*sistrum*) shaken to ward off evil. A number of statues set up in the precinct include a bronze bust

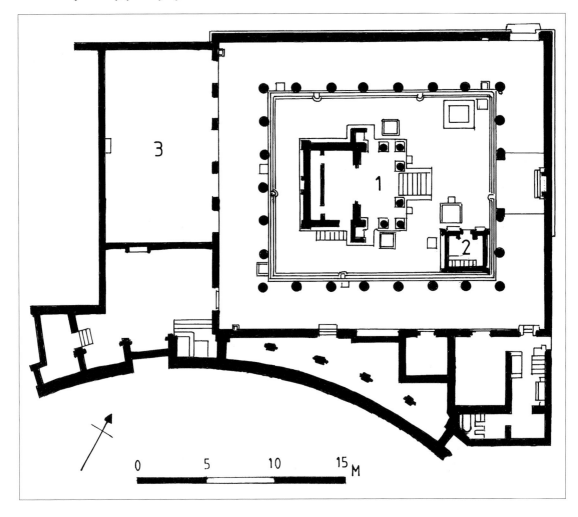

43 Plan of the temple of Isis. 1: temple; 2: *purgatorium;* 3: *ekklesiasterion. Drawing L.A. Ling*

of the actor C. Norbanus Sorex and an archaising figure of Isis, both dedicated by freedmen. These dedications reveal that the installation of the statues was sanctioned by the *decuriones* and therefore that the temple, despite the personal nature of Isiac religion, belonged to the city. Civic interest would help to explain why the council was happy to adopt the six-year-old Celsinus into its number.

The last cults to appear on the Pompeian scene were those connected with the emperor. While Rome's eastern provinces, accustomed to regarding the Hellenistic kings as gods, readily accorded divine status to the emperor, even during his lifetime, there was much greater caution in Italy and the west. Augustus in particular, mindful of Republican sentiment and of the fate of his adoptive father Julius Caesar, discouraged direct worship, preferring devotion to be directed to his spirit or his protecting fortune. Thus the temples of Fortuna

Augusta and the Genius of Augustus mentioned in Chapter 4. The former, built
by M. Tullius at the corner of Via del Foro and Via di Nola, adopted the standard
format of a *cella* fronted by a deep columnar porch, the whole raised on a high
podium; but an unusual feature, recalling the temple of Jupiter, was the placing
of the altar on a platform part-way up the entrance stairs, which split to form a
separate arm on either side of it. In the back wall of the *cella* was a two-column
aedicula (pavilion) set in an apse which would have contained a statue of Fortuna,
and in the side walls were pairs of niches for honorary statues. The cult was
supervised by *ministri* (attendants) of Fortuna Augusta who were evidently slaves
or freedmen; the establishment of the office, and thus of the cult itself, is dated
by an inscription of AD 3 which refers to the 'first *ministri*'.[13]

The temple of the Genius of Augustus, which has been identified with the so-
called Temple of Vespasian on the east side of the forum, was a different kind of
building, consisting of an open court, with an altar at the middle and a small shrine
on a podium projecting from the back wall. The reliefs on the altar, which seems to
have been repaired after the earthquake of 62, are replete with Augustan imagery;
they feature a sacrificial scene (*44*) in which the style of the figures clearly points
to the Augustan period, and the chief sacrificant has Augustus' portrait features,

44 Sacrificial relief on the altar in the temple of the Genius of Augustus. Soon after 7 BC. *Photograph
M. Thatcher (Ward-Perkins collection)*

while on the back face is a crown of oak leaves flanked by a pair of laurel trees – an unmistakable reference to honours voted to Augustus in 27 BC.[14]

A third building which may have been linked with the imperial cult is the so-called Temple of the Public Lares.[15] This was similar to the temple of the Genius of Augustus, in that it consisted of an open court with an altar at the centre and a focal *aedicula* at the rear; but the large apse in which this *aedicula* was set, the play of large recesses and small niches in the side walls, and the framing pilasters and screens of columns which enlivened the surfaces, gave the building a more complex and restless movement than found in any other Pompeian monument. The decoration was completed by an *opus sectile* pavement and by marble veneer on the walls. The avant-garde style points to a date round the middle of the first century AD, possibly even after the earthquake of 62. If this was indeed a building devoted to the imperial cult, it is possible that the niches contained statues of the Julio-Claudian emperors, rather like the similar galleries of portraits in other cities of Italy and the provinces.

So far we have dealt with public temples of various forms. But religion was not confined to formal religious buildings; it was also practised in the streets and in the home.[16] Altars at street corners, often associated with paintings or sculptures of deities, attest to the all-pervasive nature of religion. And similar shrines are found in shops, workshops and houses, protecting the activities of everyday life. The deities represented in these domestic shrines are often the same as in the public temples, with Bacchus, Venus and Heracles particularly favoured; but others not yet mentioned make an appearance, such as Mercury (Hermes), important as a god of tradesmen. Common to all houses are the Lares Familiares, protectors of the household, whose shrines are found in kitchens as well as the public parts of the house (45). They are represented as pairs of dancing figures in short tunics, generally pouring an offering of wine from a drinking horn (*rhyton*) into a libation dish (*patera*) or *situla*, and are frequently accompanied by a figure in a toga representing the *genius* of the *paterfamilias* (head of the household) and by a snake or snakes which seem to have acted as benevolent spirits protecting the house from evil (46).

Related to the cult of the household Lares is that of the Lares Compitales ('gods of the crossroads'), who guarded districts of the city. From 7 BC their worship was linked with the protecting gods of the emperor and they became known as Lares Augusti; the coordination of this cult was entrusted to *magistri* and *ministri vici* ('overseers and attendants of the parish') who were respectively often freedmen and either freedmen or slaves. The streetside shrines which they administered were decorated with depictions of Lares identical to those in houses, sometimes accompanied by a toga-clad figure which presumably depicts the *genius* of Augustus.

Alongside formal religious rites there was, of course, a vast subculture of superstition and magic practices. One manifestation of this are the ubiquitous phallic symbols, worked in tuff and terracotta, which are set in street walls or in workplaces, and even in one case carved in a paving slab in a roadway, to act as good luck charms, warding off evil spirits (*colour plate 19*). Such talismans

45 Domestic *lararium* in the *atrium* of the House of the Menander (I.10.4). Between AD 62 and 79.
Photograph R.J. Ling (Pompeii Research Committee 1993-4/33)

46 Painting of Lares and a Genius, on the *lararium* in the House of the Vettii (VI.15.1). Third quarter of first century AD. *Photograph J.-P. Adam*

were common in the ancient world. They reflect the importance of fertility to societies where infant mortality was high and prosperity depended upon the success of the harvest and the vintage.

Of Christianity, finally, there is no firm evidence. A message scrawled on a wall in a house in Region VII seems to have referred to Christians but demonstrates only that a knowledge of the new religion and its adherents, persecuted at Rome in 64, had reached Pompeii by the time of the eruption. It does not indicate that there were believers in the city.[17]

ECONOMIC LIFE

The shops and workshops which line the main streets of Pompeii bear witness to a vigorous commercial activity within the city. We can generally recognise where premises had a commercial or industrial function from their form or features. Shops have broad openings to the street, with grooves in the pavement to accommodate the shutters which closed them at night (47). Workshops – which can, of course, have retail outlets attached – are betrayed by the presence of tanks, mills, ovens, kilns and the like, or by the finding of specific types of goods which were worked or manufactured there. In some cases, especially along the eastern stretch of Via dell'Abbondanza, there remain paintings on the façade which relate to the trade in question. Unfortunately, however, the majority of commercial and industrial establishments lack finds or diagnostic features because of the ravages of post-eruption plunderers, the indifference of Bourbon excavators, or the effects of modern neglect and weathering. We know that a unit was a shop or workshop but not which particular commodities it sold or produced.

The shops naturally serviced the needs of the townspeople. On the whole they will have sold goods produced in the city and its territory, but some more

47 Shop opening (IX.7.10), with a cast of wooden shutters. *Photograph L.A. Ling*

specialised or luxury items will have been imported from further afield. Many bronze vessels, for example, may have been produced in centres celebrated for their bronze workshops, such as Capua, and glassware (*colour plate 28*) could have been imported from Puteoli, which was renowned for glass-working and even contained a quarter named after its street of glass-workers (Clivus Vitrarius). For the so-called *terra sigillata* – the red-gloss table pottery, often decorated with moulded figures and ornaments, which was fashionable in the early Empire (*colour plate 20*) – Pompeii benefited in Augustan times, as did most cities in Italy and the western provinces, from the flourishing production of Arretium (modern Arezzo) in northern Italy; but a more important source, especially after the Arretine factories closed in the Julio-Claudian period, was once again Puteoli. Some vessels were imported also from the east Mediterranean, and in the city's later years the products of southern Gaul made a first appearance: striking testimony to changing patterns of supply was afforded by a newly delivered and unopened crate of South Gaulish *sigillata* (the so-called Samian ware) found in a house on Via dell'Abbondanza (VIII.5.9).[18]

In certain areas of production, however, Pompeii was sufficiently successful to reach outside markets. Most important were viticulture and other forms of cropfarming, particularly (as in the area today) the growing of fruit and vegetables. Here the fertile, well-drained volcanic soil and the mild climate of the region were the determining factors; moreover, the city's position at a node of land communications and her command of a sea port gave her the advantage of ready access to trade-routes.

There is frequent testimony in the ancient sources to the importance of wine production in the Vesuvius region. Strabo, writing in the time of Augustus, compares the fertility of the soil with that around Etna, 'favourable to vines', and Martial reports that Vesuvius was verdant with vines before the eruption of 79 (*colour plate 21*).[19] Vesuvian wines were sufficiently well known to get mentions in the pages of Pliny's *Natural History*, as well as in the agricultural writers. One type of vine was actually called 'Pompeiana' (though its more common name was 'Murgentina' after a city in Sicily); another grown in the area was 'Horconia', a name sometimes assumed to be derived, or corrupted, from the Pompeian family Holconia. According to Pliny, Pompeian wines ceased to improve after 10 years, and an evening tipple tended to induce a hangover which lasted halfway through the following day. Despite these drawbacks, they evidently enjoyed wide success. Amphorae bearing the stamp of the early Augustan producer L. Eumachius have been found at Rome's port of Ostia and as far afield as Carthage, Gaul and Spain. The extent of wine production is confirmed by the excavations of farms round Pompeii, almost all of which have revealed wine presses (*48*) and yards with rows of large *dolia* (storage jars) set in the ground to act as fermentation vats. In the small villa at Boscoreale best known for its silver treasure, for instance, there were 84 *dolia*, of which 72 were for wine; the potential capacity of these was over 90,000 litres, which would be consonant (allowing for a little cultivation

48 Reconstructed wine-press in the Villa of the Mysteries. The beam decorated with a ram's head is drawn down by tightening the rope, so as to exert pressure on a box containing the grapes. *Photograph R.J. Ling 100/20*

of cereals, vegetables and fruit as well) with a holding in the range of 10-15ha (25-37 acres). At another rural site, recent excavations have revealed not just the farm building but also part of the surrounding vineyard (*49*); and we now know that there were small commercial vineyards even within the walls of the city.[20]

Of the vegetables grown at Pompeii, two – cabbages and onions – were well enough known to have varieties named 'Pompeian': the agricultural writer Columella recommends the onions in particular.[21] Other vegetables may well have been grown for more than local consumption, though positive evidence is lacking. Among those referred to in Pompeian graffiti or labels on amphorae, or identified from carbonised material recovered either at Pompeii or at Herculaneum, are broad beans, lentils, chickpeas and various legumes. In urban contexts a desire to get the maximum use from the available plots – not to mention the fertility of the soil which permitted dense planting – resulted in vegetables being intercultivated among vines or trees.

Fruits identified from carbonised remains include almonds, figs, filberts, walnuts, cherries, apples, pears, peaches and pomegranates. Others whose presence can

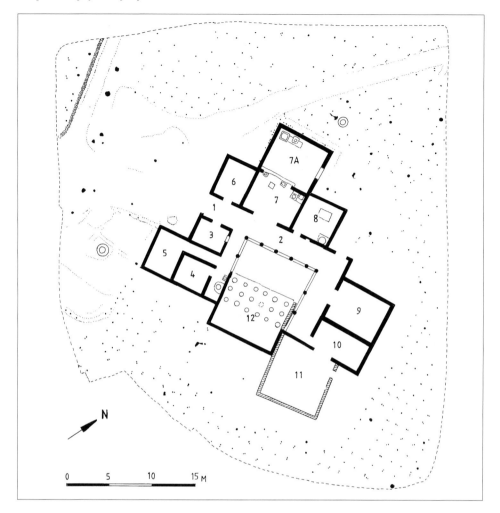

49 Excavation of a small farm at Boscoreale. 1: entrance; 2: portico; 3-5: living rooms; 6: store room; 7-7A wine factory; 8: kitchen; 9: dining room; 10: hay store; 11: threshing floor; 12: yard with fermentation vats. The surrounding vineyards were recognised from regular rows of root cavities. Larger cavities indicated the presence of trees (four walnuts, four figs, a peach, two planes, two pines, and 14 almonds or olives). *Drawing R.J. Ling, after S. De Caro,* La villa rustica in località Villa Regina a Boscoreale *(1994)*

be deduced from surviving wood or from representations in wall-paintings are lemons and plums. Olives, too, though rare in the Pompeii region today, are now known to have been widely grown there in antiquity. Their oil was essential not just for culinary purposes but also as a fuel in lamps. Several of the *dolia* found in the *villa rustica* at Boscoreale were intended for oil. Whether Pompeii produced oil for more than local sale is unknown, but she was renowned for her oil mills. Cato the Elder in his book *On Agriculture* specifically includes them among his recommended brands.[22]

One other product for which Pompeii was famed (Pliny puts it among the most highly acclaimed varieties of the Empire) is a 'fruit of the sea' – the fish sauce *garum*.[23] This condiment, otherwise known by the Latin name *liquamen*, was produced from extracts of various fish allowed to ferment for periods in the sun and was graded, rather like wine, according to quality. The best quality was a luxury item *gari flos* ('the flower of *garum*'), but we also hear of *liquamen optimum* ('finest *liquamen*'). One of the workshops in which the sauce was prepared has been excavated at Pompeii I.12.8, and the house of A. Umbricius Scaurus, the city's leading manufacturer, is on the western margins: the owner's pride in his products is demonstrated in the mosaic pavement of his *atrium*, which was decorated at the corners of the *impluvium* with representations of jars labelled '*liqua(minis) flos*' ('the flower of *liquamen*') and '*g(ari) f(los) scom(bri) Scauri*' ('Scaurus' flower of *garum*, made from mackerel'). Surviving jars with workshop labels, found in many parts of the city, reveal that Scaurus had a number of establishments operated by a network of slaves, freedmen and perhaps family members. His jars have turned up at Herculaneum and in a shipwreck off Fos-sur-Mer in southern France, while an amphora labelled *gar(um) Pompeianum* is known at Rome. Here, certainly, was a product that had more than local currency.

Another form of production in which Pompeii has been thought to be more than self-sufficient is that of woollen cloth. A study by Walter O. Moeller has argued that it was one of the main industries of the city and an important source of wealth. That viewpoint has been challenged by W. Jongman, who believes that spinning and weaving were essentially domestic activities and that Pompeian textile production never rose above the level of a local service industry.[24] The truth probably lies somewhere between the two extremes, but Jongman's more cautious assessment of the situation seems to be nearer the truth. Sheep were raised throughout Italy for their meat, milk, manure and wool, and it is likely that the Pompeii area was no exception. Seneca, indeed, reports that 'hundreds' of sheep perished there in the earthquake of 62. On the other hand, to have grazed large flocks on the fertile volcanic soil of the Sarno plain and the foothills of Vesuvius would have been an uneconomic use of land ideally suited to viticulture and fruit-growing: we must assume that most farms in the immediate vicinity of the city kept few sheep, and that any large-scale grazing took place on the higher slopes of Vesuvius or, more probably, on the limestone mountains to the south of the Sarno and further up the valley. This would mean that the bulk of any wool processed at Pompeii was imported from the territory of neighbouring cities such as Nuceria. But the chief argument against the theory that Pompeii produced woollen cloth in quantity is the lack of clear evidence for major weaving establishments. While loom-weights have turned up in almost every house that has been excavated, they normally occur only in ones and twos. There are some larger concentrations, and three houses have produced assemblages of more than 50 weights, but in each case these were found in one place and testify to no more than the presence of a single warp–weighted loom (or possibly two): at the most they point to small-scale domestic weaving such as would be found in any city. It is significant that there is only one Pompeian graffito so far known which refers specifically to a *textor* (weaver). If cloth production was the basis of a flourishing industry, one would have expected the practitioners of the craft to be more prominent in the epigraphic record.

There were certainly workshops for the processing of wool and the cleaning of cloth, but these may represent little more than a service industry. Among the establishments that have been recognised is a fullery at VI.8.20 where stalls for the treading of cloth, tanks for rinsing it, and an upstairs terrace for drying it

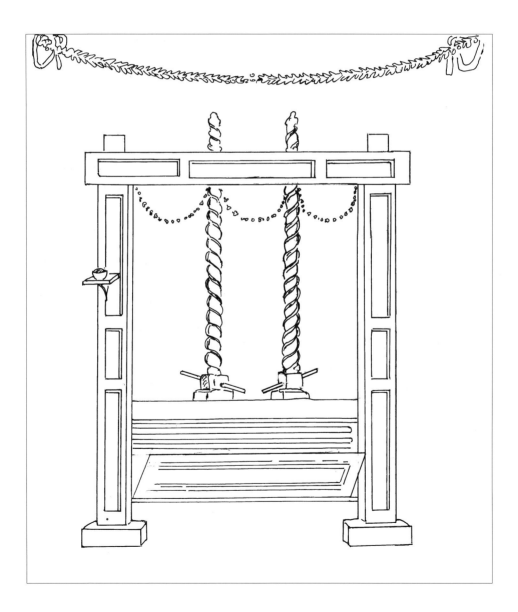

were installed in the peristyle of an old house converted to industrial use. From a pillar in this peristyle come paintings which illustrate the various processes involved: particularly interesting are representations of a clothes press and of a hemispherical 'cage' of canes on which garments were spread to be whitened with sulphur fumes (*50*). Another, smaller fullery was that ascribed to Stephanus on Via dell'Abbondanza (I.6.7). This contained similar treading stalls and rinsing tanks (including one created by adapting the *impluvium* in the *atrium*) and sported an election manifesto of the fullers on its street façade. Further establishments connected with cloth processing are a dye works at I.8.19, identified from four lead cauldrons over small furnaces which could have been used to heat the

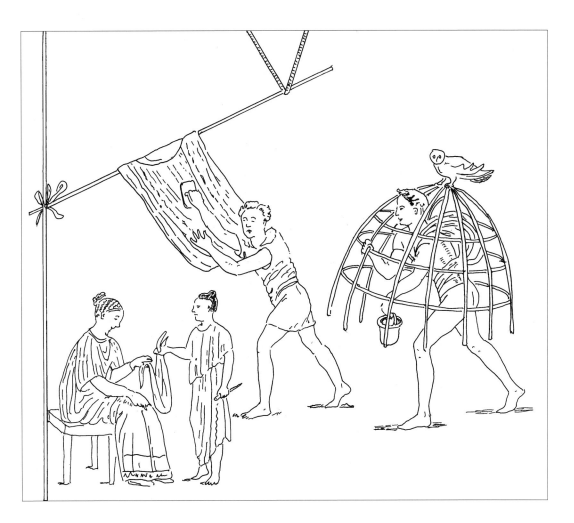

50 Paintings from a pillar in the peristyle of the fullery VI.8.20: (a) *Opposite* A wooden clothes press; (b) *Above* Cleaning operations (a worker cards material hung over a line, another brings a cage and a bucket of sulphur for use in a whitening process, and a woman examines a piece of cloth handed her by a maid). Naples Museum 9774. *Drawings L.A. Ling*

colouring solutions, and the textile factory of Verecundus (IX.7.7), identified from a painted 'shop sign' of workers combing fleeces and making felt. Verecundus himself, duly labelled, holds up a finished cloak for public inspection. This last painting is disfigured by an election appeal on behalf of the 'felt-makers' (*coactiliarii*, rendered in the local dialect as *quactiliari*), and a few doors along is another similar manifesto, as well as one sponsored by the dyers (*infectores*).

All this demonstrates that there were businesses for the cleaning and colouring of cloth, but not that they formed part of an industry that brought substantial income into the city. Much of the work of the establishments that Moeller has identified was certainly in the restoration of old clothing: they were the ancient counterparts of modern dry cleaners. More important, some of Moeller's identifications are based on flimsy evidence, such as graffiti of uncertain significance or the mere presence of furnaces and tanks – apparatus which could have been used in various manufacturing processes unconnected with textiles. We should think of Pompeii's cloth producers primarily as catering to the needs of the city and its *territorium*, not as cogs in a major export operation.

Many other establishments in the city were unequivocally those of local service industries. Such are the bakeries, identifiable from the mills used to grind grain into flour and from the ovens in which the loaves were baked. A good example is at VII.2.22 (*colour plate 22*), where a yard paved with basalt slabs contains four grain mills in a row, each constructed in the standard format of two components of lava: a hollow hourglass-shaped element (the *catillus*) fitted over a conical element (the *meta*) which was set on a circular pedestal with a raised lip round the edge. Drawn by a donkey, the *catillus* rotated round the *meta*, and grain poured into the upper cavity passed into the lower part, where it was ground into flour by the friction between the two elements, emerging at the bottom to be collected in the surrounding trough. To the right of the mills, against the bakery wall, was a series of masonry supports for wooden benches on which assistants kneaded the dough, and to the left was a domed oven with an arched opening giving access to the floor on which the fire was lit and the bread was baked. Further rooms provided storage space for sacks of grain and the finished loaves, but this particular bakery had no shop attached: presumably it was the property of a wholesale producer who delivered his goods to outlets elsewhere (including street-sellers or market traders) or even directly to private customers. Other bakeries, by contrast, had their own retail outlets. A well-known painting from Pompeii VIII.3.30 (*51*) is now thought to represent a free distribution of bread by a public benefactor, but it gives a good impression of what a baker's shop may have looked like, with piles of round loaves laid out on the counter and on shelves at the back.

Far more numerous than the bakeries are the various food and drink shops. These are recognisable from their distinctive counters, regularly L-shaped in form, with one arm across the broad street entrance and the other extending inwards, so that the salesman or woman could serve both passers-by in the street

51 Painting of a distribution of loaves, from the *tablinum* of VII.3.30. 62 x 53cm. Naples Museum 9071. *Photograph E. de Maré*

and other customers inside the shop. The counters contained inset *dolia*, and there was often a small stove at the end of the inner arm on which hot drinks could be prepared (*52*). The contents of the *dolia* have rarely been preserved or observed, but are likely to have been nuts, fruits, vegetables and the like. What we would call 'inns' or 'taverns' had a similar bar at the entrance, but also offered accommodation or provided back rooms for gaming and other entertainments. The criteria for distinguishing such establishments from simple food and drink

52 Above Top of an L-shaped counter containing inset *dolia* (storage jars). At the end is a recess that would have housed a small stove. Food and drink shop at I.2.18. *Photograph L.A. Ling*

53 Opposite above Dice-players: painting in a tavern (VI.10.1, room B). *Photograph German Archaeological Institute Rome 31.1751*

54 Opposite below Relief of a builder's tools, from a street wall at the corner of VII.15. Included are a plumb-bob (?), a shovel (?), a builder's level, a float or mortar-board, the head of a mason's hammer, and a chisel. At the top, roughly incised, was the inscription DIOGENES STRVCTOR ('Diogenes the builder'). 34.5 x 63.5cm. Pompeii Antiquarium 2254. *Photograph R.J. Ling 77/20*

shops with the shopkeeper's living quarters at the rear are painted inscriptions describing the premises as a *hospitium* (inn) or the occupier as a *caupo* or *copo* (pub landlord) and graffiti or paintings referring to the activities which took place there. An interesting series of paintings in a hostelry at VI.10.1 shows customers eating and drinking, having their cups refilled, and tossing dice at a table (*53*); there is also a scene of wine being delivered by a donkey-drawn wagon. Some inns even displayed their own pictorial emblems, like the inn signs of modern Britain: the *hospitium* of Sittius, for example, had a painted elephant on its front wall, the *caupona* of Euxinus a phoenix.

Other service industries for which there was a regular need were building (*54*), painting, and other forms of decorating. The need was, of course, especially acute in the last years, when there was hardly a structure in the city that was not undergoing restoration as a result of the earthquake of 62.

Finally, we must mention prostitution. Here the extent of demand and supply has often been exaggerated. This applies even to recent publications, one of which includes a catalogue of 41 brothels liberally sprinkled in most parts of the city – surely a gross case of overkill.[25] Many of the supposed identifications depend, in fact, upon such ambiguous evidence as erotic or pornographic graffiti on neighbouring street walls, and must be rejected. Some inns doubtless offered rooms for assignations, but there are few establishments which are unequivocally recognisable as *lupanaria* (brothels). A clear exception is a bordello in a back street near the Stabian Baths (VII.12.18-20), where each of a series of identical small chambers containing masonry beds has, over its doorway, a painting of a couple making love. These paintings can only have been advertisements of the delights to be had within – delights which were commemorated in numerous graffiti on the walls.

Further evidence of the economic life of the city comes from the public buildings which were provided for tradesmen. Most important of these was the Macellum, or food market, a courtyard building at the north-east corner of the forum (*55*). At the centre of the court was a circular pavilion with a supply of running water, used for the washing of fish, the scales and bones of which were discovered by the excavators. Along the south side lay a range of shops, while further shops faced the streets to the north and west. Remains of fruits, nuts and cereals bear witness to the commodities on offer. At the south-east corner was a room devoted to the sale of meat and fish, and in the middle of the east side was a shrine for the imperial cult, installed in the Julio-Claudian reconstruction.[26]

On the opposite side of the forum a portico fronted by eight brick-faced pillars is thought to have been the Forum Olitorium, a market for the sale of cereals and dry vegetables. The identification is based on the proximity of a measuring table, set in a recess immediately to the south. This consisted of two limestone slabs, one above the other, the lower containing nine cup-shaped cavities, and the upper three, all labelled with standard measures of capacity so that traders could check that they had the correct quantities of grain etc. An earlier system

55 Macellum: general view of the interior. *Photograph R.J. Ling 112/36*

of measurements dating from the Samnite period had been replaced by new standards in Augustan times, with the cavities being recut accordingly.

One last building which is thought by many to have had a commercial function is the Building of Eumachia, set in the angle formed by the forum and the north side of Via dell'Abbondanza. This imposing edifice consisted of three main elements, all listed in the donor Eumachia's dedicatory inscription: a broad and deep porch or vestibule (*chalcidicum*), a colonnaded court (*porticus*), and an enclosing corridor or cryptoportico (*crypta*). The argument for commercial use hinges on a second inscription, recording that a statue of Eumachia which stood in the back corridor was set up by fullers. This has prompted suggestions that the building was a guild hall of the fullers or a cloth exchange, with the enclosing corridor used for storage, the central court for cleaning and rinsing the materials, and the vestibule, which contained open-fronted tribunals reached by stairways, for auctions. But the fact that the fullers honoured Eumachia with a statue proves nothing about the function of the building, and there are no architectural or other features that point unequivocally to a connection with the textile industry, or indeed with any other form of production or exchange. A recent idea that the building served as a slave market is equally difficult to substantiate.[27] The tenor of the dedicatory inscription, which identifies Eumachia as a 'public priestess' and says that she dedicated her *chalcidicum*, *crypta* and *porticus* to Concordia Augusta and Pietas, concepts associated with the ideology of the imperial court, implies that this was not a commercial building, but a civic or religious one. The presence in the *chalcidicum* of statues and inscriptions apparently inspired by the iconographic programme of the Forum of Augustus in Rome points the same way. At the rear of the internal court a large apse perhaps contained a statue of Concordia. We cannot assign a specific role, but may suspect that the Building of Eumachia was used for the performance of religious ceremonies or the transaction of public business of some kind. When not in use for these purposes, it may have served, like the public porticoes in Rome, as a place where people could relax, seek shelter from sun or rain, and perhaps admire works of art no longer preserved.

SOCIAL LIFE

If we leave aside the more intimate entertainments of the taverns and brothels, there were three main social activities available at Pompeii: going to the public baths, attending performances in the theatre, and watching the shows in the amphitheatre.

The public baths played a major role in the life of Pompeii, as they did in Rome itself and countless other cities, because of their importance to public hygiene. While some of the wealthier citizens had bath suites in their houses, the vast majority of the population enjoyed no such advantage, and going to the public baths was a virtual necessity. For this reason admission fees were minimal, and no one, however poor, was excluded. This meant, in turn, that the baths became a social centre second to none: everyone met there to pass the time and exchange the latest gossip.

The mode of bathing anticipated that of the later Turkish baths, with rooms of graded heat (cold, warm and hot) which offered the bather the opportunity to cleanse the pores by sweating and to immerse himself or herself in hot and cold plunge baths. Although there were no hard and fast rules, a normal procedure would be to head for the hottest room first, sweat out impurities, rinse the body in a hot bath, then return to the cold room for the invigorating tonic of a cold dip. But, for the younger and fitter clients, there was also the opportunity for exercise – running, wrestling or playing ball games – in the attached *palaestra*, a feature clearly inspired by Greek *gymnasia* (pp. 44–5).

The baths of Pompeii enable us to follow the technological development of bathing in Italy from its beginnings to the mature accomplishments of the Imperial age. The earliest establishment seems to have been the centrally placed

56 Stabian Baths, *palaestra* (exercise court). *Photograph R.J. Ling 113/9*

Stabian Baths (*56*).[28] Here excavations by Hans Eschebach have identified a series of rooms containing Greek-style hip-baths which may go back to the fourth century BC. But the first developed complex of Roman type is assigned to the second century, when two sets of heated rooms, one for men and one for women, were laid out back to back with a furnace between them and a *palaestra* alongside them. In this early stage water was winched up from a well and collected in cisterns and a rooftop reservoir, as Pompeii was not yet provided with running water.

With the planting of the Roman colony, the amenities in the Stabian Baths were improved by the addition of a circular room of dry heat (*laconicum*) and a room for scraping the body clean after exercise (*destrictarium*). But, perhaps because of dissatisfaction with the more out-of-date features of the baths and because of an increased demand for bathing facilities in the wake of the colonisation, it was decided to construct a new complex, the Forum Baths (*24*). This was provided with a *laconicum* from the outset and may already have received running water, which was collected in a huge tank in the neighbouring *insula*. It was also part of a complex which included shops and bars, the rents from which doubtless helped to pay for the upkeep of the establishment. In terms of technical developments the hot room (*caldarium*) was now provided with a fully fledged underfloor and wall-cavity heating system (the hollow walls perhaps already achieved with *tegulae mammatae*) of the kind which subsequently became standard in Roman Italy; but the warm room (*tepidarium*), at least in the men's section, relied solely upon a charcoal brazier, which was still the only form of heating available in this room in AD 79.

During the subsequent 150 years of their existence the Stabian and Forum Baths saw further refinements, as fashions changed and technologies advanced. In the Augustan period, the baths were linked to the water mains supplied by the newly built aqueduct. At the same time, the *laconicum*, with its cumbersome system of heating based on a brazier and a bronze disc which was lowered or raised to regulate the supply of air through a central opening in its conical dome, was adapted to become a cold room (*frigidarium*) occupied by a plunge bath. The Stabian Baths were also expanded westwards to incorporate a plot previously occupied by a private house, and the newly acquired land was utilised for the addition of an open-air swimming pool. But the old baths always remained ill-lit, because the need to retain heat precluded the use of large windows. Apart from the central skylight of the *frigidarium*, and similar small roof openings in the other rooms, there was no source of natural illumination. This situation began to change in the Imperial period with improvements in heating technology and in the production of window glass. Already the comparatively small Suburban Baths, datable to Julio-Claudian times, incorporated some of the new developments. The Central Baths, constructed after the earthquake of 62 but never finished, were destined to be a fully fledged imperial-style bath building, with chambers lit by large windows facing south-west to exploit the afternoon sunshine.[29] These windows could have been filled with panes of glass set in metal or wooden grilles, but the radiant heat imparted by new systems of wall-flues, incorporating hollow box tiles, may have been sufficiently effective to render window glass almost superfluous. A further change in these incomplete baths was the lack of separate suites for men and women. Assuming that the Central Baths were intended to cater for both sexes, we must conclude that, as in the baths at the mining settlement of Vipasca in Portugal, whose arrangements are recorded in a surviving inscription,[30] the women would have attended in the morning (from daybreak to the seventh hour of the day, i.e. about 1 p.m.) and the men in the afternoon (from the eighth hour to sunset).

The Central Baths never, however, came into service, and the essential arrangements of Pompeian bathing in the city's later years remained those of the Forum and Stabian Baths. We may take as an example the Forum Baths (*24*), which had apparently been restored after the damage inflicted in AD 62. Here the men's section consisted of a changing room (*apodyterium*) off which opened the circular *frigidarium*, the *tepidarium* and the *caldarium*. The *apodyterium*

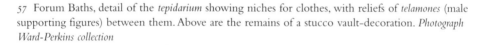

57 Forum Baths, detail of the tepidarium *showing niches for clothes, with reliefs of* telamones *(male supporting figures) between them. Above are the remains of a stucco vault-decoration. Photograph Ward-Perkins collection*

contained benches along the walls on which bathers could sit, but there were none of the normal niches for clothes to be stored; these must have been replaced by wooden shelves, the nail holes for which are still visible. The *tepidarium*, by contrast, preserves niches between which are terracotta reliefs of *telamones* (male supporting figures) whose bent arms appear to carry the cornice at the spring of the vault (57); this vault is decorated with a coloured stucco decoration datable to the post-earthquake repair. The *caldarium*, following a standard format, terminates at one end in an apse containing a marble wash-basin (*labrum*) while at the other end is a rectangular bathtub provided with hot water from a boiler in the adjacent furnace room (*praefurnium*). The vault has stucco fluting designed to channel condensation down to the side walls rather than leaving it to drip on the bathers. The women's baths, ranged on the other side of the *praefurnium*, but reached by a separate street entrance, are similar to the men's but smaller and simpler, with the

58 Statue of Doryphorus (spear-bearer) from the Samnite Palaestra. Such statues, copied from a famous fifth-century BC bronze by Polyclitus, were regularly exhibited in Greek *gymnasia*. Height 2.12 m. Naples Museum 6011. *Photograph University of Manchester, Art History collection (Anderson 23079)*

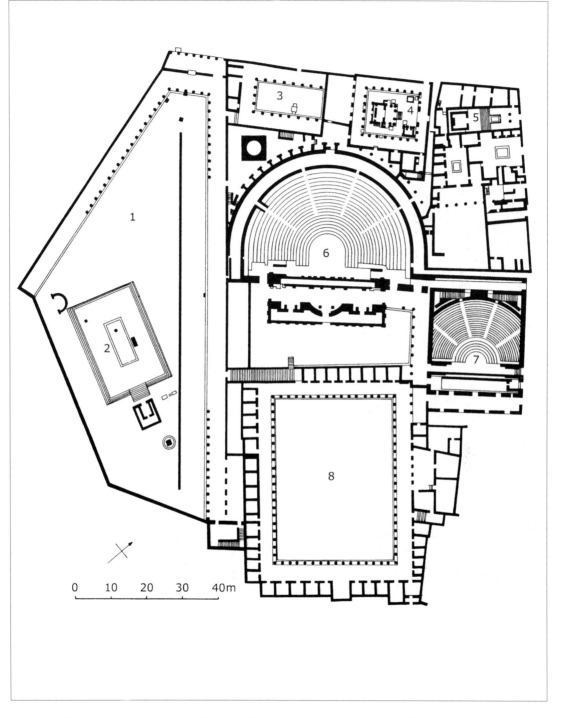

59 Plan of the theatre quarter. 1: Triangular Forum; 2: temple of Minerva and Heracles (Doric
temple); 3: Samnite Palaestra; 4: temple of Isis; 5: temple of Aesculapius(?); 6: large theatre; 7: small
(covered) theatre; 8: gladiators' barracks (formerly *gymnasium?*). *After J.B. Ward-Perkins and A. Claridge,*
Pompeii AD 79 *(1976)*

cold-water plunge bath incorporated within the changing room rather than set in a separate chamber. Finally, the *palaestra*, framed by colonnades, was reached by a passage from the men's *apodyterium*, as well as having separate street entrances, both from the east and from the west.

The same arrangements are mirrored in the Stabian Baths, apparently not fully operational in AD 79. There were also establishments in the city which preserved the Greek emphasis upon physical exercise without the accompanying baths. The so-called Samnite Palaestra, with its statue inspired by the spear-bearer of Polyclitus (*58*), a standard emblem of Greek *gymnasia*, is the clearest example, but this was limited in size, and, as noted in Chapter 2, the large colonnaded piazza behind the theatre may have been designed as a full-scale *gymnasium* of Hellenistic type. It is also possible that the Triangular Forum could have been used for running races in the Samnite period, as what appears to be a track is marked out adjacent to the east portico.[31] But these early athletic facilities were dwarfed by the Large Palaestra built in Augustan times (*colour plate 8*). Occupying a space equal to six *insulae* next to the amphitheatre, and enclosed on three sides by long colonnades (36 on north and south, 48 on the west) and on the fourth by a plain wall, this was probably intended to cater primarily for the training of the youth corps established by the emperor and only secondarily for the amusement of the general public.

The second principal social activity available to Pompeians was visiting the theatre. When first built in the second century BC, the Pompeian theatre (*59, colour plate 23*) – generally called the 'large theatre' to distinguish it from the 'small' or 'covered theatre' – was smaller than at present, and its auditorium (*cavea*), slightly greater than a semicircle, was independent of the stage building. During subsequent restorations, notably in Augustan times (see Chapter 4), the *cavea* was heightened and extended, with the construction of a continuous vaulted passage (*crypta*) to carry additional rows of seats at the rear, while the passages between the *cavea* and the stage were roofed over to provide extra places at the sides, including privileged viewing enclosures (*tribunalia*) similar to the boxes in a modern theatre. The Augustan restoration probably also involved replacing the old seats of volcanic tuff with new ones of marble. In the final version of the auditorium the central zone, or *media cavea*, corresponding to the 'circle' of a modern theatre, consisted of 20 rows of seats, and the upper zone, or *summa cavea*, corresponding to our 'gallery', of a further four rows. Distribution within the *media cavea* (what happened in the *summa cavea* is unknown) was by six stairways which descended from the *crypta* and divided the seating into five wedge-shaped sectors (*cunei*). At the bottom of the auditorium, in the position of the modern 'stalls', were four rows of broad and shallow steps (*ima cavea*) for the honorary thrones (*bisellia*) of the decurions and other local dignitaries.

The stage, 1m high and 6.60m from front to back, had fittings near the front for the curtain, or *siparium*, which was lowered at the start of performances and raised at the end. At the rear, forming the front of the long, narrow stage building,

60 Painting of a scene from a comedy. The figure in the doorway at the left is wearing a theatrical mask characteristic of an old slave. 32 x 65cm. House of the Centenary (IX.8.6), *atrium* (now illegible). *Photograph German Archaeological Institute Rome 53.633*

was a monumental façade of two storeys enlivened by columns and statues, the result probably of the same Augustan restoration that saw the modernisation of the *cavea*. The principal features were an apsidal recess at the centre and a pair of rectangular ones at the sides; these contained the three traditional entrances of Greek and Roman theatrical backdrops.

We have no direct evidence as to what types of performances were staged in the theatre. They no doubt included farces of Italian origin, the so-called *fabulae Atellanae*, featuring stock characters such as Maccus (the buffoon), Bucco (the loud-mouthed lout), Pappus (the old man who always gets bamboozled) and Dossennus (the glutton). There may also have been 'mimes', a more varied form of farce, and 'pantomimes', entertainments in which dancers re-enacted mythological themes. But, to judge from the theatrical scenes depicted in the wall-paintings of Pompeian houses, notably the House of the Theatrical Panels and the House of the Centenary (*60*), from the portraits of the tragic and comic playwrights

Euripides and Menander (*colour plate 24*) painted in the so-called House of the Menander, and from the theatrical masks which are a favourite motif not only in Pompeii's paintings but also in decorative sculpture, an important part of the repertory must have remained the dramas of ancient Greece. The better-educated citizens, at least, were aficionados of the classics of the stage.

The function of the small theatre, built in the first years of the colony (see Chapter 3), is somewhat less clear. This building repeats the large theatre's format of a shell-like auditorium facing a stage, but the semicircular bank of seating is truncated at each side by the walls of a huge rectangular hall which encloses and covers the complex. Access to the upper rows of seats was via staircases in the back corners. The original appearance of the two monuments, despite the generic resemblance suggested by photographs which show their present ruined state, would have been radically different. The large theatre was open to the sky, and the curving lines of its *cavea* dominated the design; the small theatre, by contrast, was a rectangular building with a saddle roof. There was also a pronounced difference in size. It is estimated that the large theatre could have accommodated between 3,500 and 5,000 spectators, whereas the capacity of the small one was no more than 1,000-1,500.

Normally, in Greek contexts, small covered theatres are classified as *odeia* and identified as halls for musical performances or poetry readings. But at least two cities of the Hellenistic period, Priene and Miletus, both on the west coast of Asia Minor, employed a similar formula for their council chambers. A recent theory (see Chapter 3) has proposed that Pompeii's covered theatre was designed to serve as the assembly hall of the Roman colonists. However, this cannot have remained its exclusive function, and the treatment of the *ima cavea* and *tribunalia*, both marked out as places of privileged viewing, is reminiscent of the arrangements in the large theatre. One must conclude that the small theatre, while sometimes used for political and other meetings, doubled as a venue for entertainments of more restricted appeal than those staged in the large theatre. The fact that it was roofed, moreover, meant that it was available all year round, regardless of weather. On certain occasions it may have served as a substitute location, albeit of reduced capacity, when events scheduled for the large theatre were rained off.

The third of the major social activities available to Pompeians – and by far the most popular – was attending the shows in the amphitheatre.[32] These consisted of two main entertainments: combats between pairs of gladiators (*colour plate 25*), each equipped with arms which characterised different categories of fighter, and confrontations between huntsmen (*venatores*) and wild animals. The events were assembled in as varied and lavish a pattern as possible, often lasting for two, three or even more days, and they were advertised, like the election campaigns, by posters painted on street walls. It is significant that these posters publicised the same prominent citizens who had canvassed support in the election manifestoes, and who now demonstrated that they were carrying out their civic duties in providing entertainments – and thus ensured public acclamation and future support. A typical poster reads: 'Cn. Alleius Nigidius Maius, *quinquennalis*, is providing thirty pairs of gladiators and their substitutes; they will fight at Pompeii on 24, 25 and 26 November. There will be a hunt. Long live Maius the *quinquennalis*.' Sometimes the sponsor seems to have embellished the events with further attractions, including distributions of gifts of fruit or money. More frequent was the promise of *vela* (awnings to provide shade) and *sparsiones* (the sprinkling of water or perfumes), much appreciated palliatives to the heat of the afternoon sun.

The best gladiators were professional performers who travelled from city to city. Grouped in schools or *ludi*, the most famous of which were imperial ones based at Capua, they were managed by impresarios called *lanistae* who probably let them out to the local sponsors or entered into contracts to organise the shows on their behalf. Other gladiators were independent operators or the property of individual masters, and some of them were clearly based in Pompeii. One house in the northern part of the city, the so-called Gladiators' Barracks, seems from graffiti to have been occupied for a time by a number of gladiators. The quadriportico behind the theatre was in the city's last years apparently converted, at least in part, into true gladiators' barracks: the *exedra* on the south side was painted with depictions of gladiatorial armour, while actual equipment, including helmets (*colour plate 26*), a shield, greaves (*colour plate 27*), shoulder protectors, a sword and a pair of daggers, was found stored in the neighbouring rooms.

The life of a gladiator was, of course, perilous and likely to be curtailed any time that he took up arms in the arena; for this reason many of the performers were slaves or criminals conscripted for the purpose, while others were probably down-and-outs who had nothing better to hope for and saw the shows as a means to secure popular adulation (and perhaps ultimately, in the event of success, sufficient wealth to retire from the sport). It would be wrong, however, to assume that duels in the Pompeian amphitheatre usually ended in the death of one of the combatants. Good gladiators were a valuable commodity, and the spectators, who had the final say as to whether a defeated protagonist should be dispatched, may well have been disposed or encouraged to exercise clemency. Certainly some gladiators made regular appearances and acquired something of the celebrity status of modern footballers or pop stars. Witness to this perhaps are the graffiti that refer to the 'Thracian' Celadus as *puellarum decus* or *suspirium puellarum* ('glory' or 'heart-throb of the girls') and describe Crescens the *retiarius* (a gladiator who fought with a net and trident) as *puparum nocturnarum ... medicus* ('doctor of the darlings of the night').

The amphitheatre, situated at the eastern end of the city, is one of the earliest surviving examples of this purely Roman type of entertainment structure (6, 61). It displays the standard format of an elliptical arena surrounded by a continuous ramp of seating as in a modern sports stadium; but, unlike the Colosseum and other later amphitheatres, the auditorium was not supported on

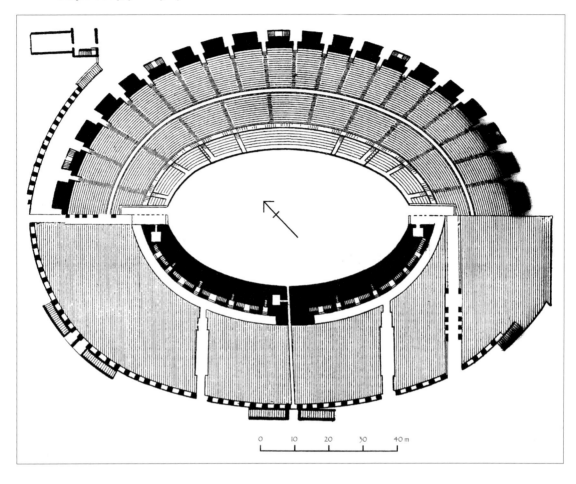

61 Plan of the amphitheatre (*c.* 70 BC). *After A. Mau,* Pompeji in Leben und Kunst *(1908)*

concrete substructures containing a network of passages and stairways but rested essentially on solid banks of earth. On the south and east, these were provided by the rampart of the old city fortifications; on the other sides they exploited the upcast obtained from excavating the arena, which lies more than 6m below the surrounding street level. The principal means of access from the exterior to the arena were a pair of sloping tunnels, one at either end, paved with basalt slabs for the passage of wheeled vehicles; the one at the north is thought to have been the *porta triumphalis* through which the gladiators and wild beasts entered, the one at the south, which turned at a right angle so as to issue within the city walls, to have been the *porta libitinensis* (the 'door of death') through which the bodies of men and animals were removed. Given the threat from wild beasts, the auditorium was separated from the arena by a high parapet (decorated with paintings of amphitheatre scenes) and access to the lower seats was via a vaulted corridor opening from the end tunnels but reached also by a pair of passages from the west. From this corridor a series of regular openings admitted spectators to the *ima cavea*, and stairways led up to the *media cavea*. To the topmost seats there was direct access by external stairways, two pairs of which converge against the north-west sector to form one of the most distinctive features of the building (*62*). The ramps carrying the stairways are pierced by arched recesses which grow taller as the steps rise, and a further series of arched recesses runs round the main structure. The piers between these recesses serve the practical purpose of buttressing the retaining wall which holds back the auditorium's earthen bank; at the same time they carry a terrace which enabled crowds to circulate outside the upper part of the auditorium. On a more mundane level, the recesses provided stations for traders who (as painted inscriptions have revealed) obtained the permission of the aediles to set up stalls on the days of the games.

As in the theatre, the decurions would have had privileged seats in the *ima cavea*, notably in the central sector on each of the long sides. The chief citizens would thus have been as conspicuous in their attendance as they were in their promotion of the shows. They also vaunted their role in funding improvements to the structure. Not only were there inscriptions commemorating the original builders but two further duovirs, the father and son C. Cuspius Pansa, were

62 Detail of the exterior (west) of the amphitheatre (*c.* 70 BC), showing one of the stairways to the top seats. *Photograph R.J. Ling*

63 View into an *atrium* house. The entrance passage leads into the *atrium* with its characteristic roof opening; behind this is the *tablinum*, and at the rear a small court containing a mosaic-decorated fountain. House of the Small Fountain (VI.8.23). *Photograph R.J. Ling 100/2*

honoured with statues set in niches in the northern entrance tunnel, probably in recognition of their role in financing repairs after the earthquake of 62. There were also inscriptions recording the names of prominent citizens who paid for the stone seats which seem to have been installed piecemeal in the *media* and *summa cavea*, gradually replacing earlier ones presumably of wood.[33] This recalls the modern practice of getting individuals to sponsor seats in theatres. Whether it was inspired by a genuine devotion to the amphitheatre or simply by a desire for self-advertisement, it testifies to the popularity of the shows and the important role that they played in social life.

DOMESTIC LIFE

Much has already been said in preceding chapters about forms of houses and how they functioned. We can here concentrate on making some general observations on domestic life in the city.

The best known and most distinctive feature of Pompeian houses is the *atrium* (*63*; cf. *30*). This central hall, with its characteristic roof opening (*compluvium*), appears in all kinds of dwellings, from modest establishments of little more than 120sq m in ground area to double-*atrium* mansions occupying most, if not all, of an *insula*. While there is a tendency to axial symmetry, with a centrally placed entrance passage at the front, an equally central *tablinum* at the rear, and a pair of identical *alae* at the sides (*15*), the number of examples that come close to the ideal is minute: the Houses of Sallust and of the Surgeon are constantly illustrated in modern books because they are virtually the only two in which a symmetrical kernel is clearly detectable. More often than not the rooms to the left of the *atrium* do not balance those to the right (and may not have done so even in the first phase of the house); and in many cases one or both side-ranges are dispensed with altogether. The *tablinum*, too, may be displaced or omitted, as in the House of the Vettii.

The more radical departures from the ideal layout are conditioned by restrictions in the size and shape of the plot available. What is surprising is that the *atrium*, being prodigal of space, should have been considered so essential that it was incorporated even in small houses. Householders were prepared to sacrifice up to a third of their ground area for the sake of having this grand conceit. One factor was certainly the role of the *compluvium* and its accompanying *impluvium* in collecting water for household use. But not every *compluvium* was designed to catch the rain, and many *impluvia* were largely ornamental, being connected to no underground cistern. We must conclude that the *atrium* had become a conventional feature. In the small houses it must have acquired the force of a status symbol, designed to mimic the lofty halls of the great houses where it functioned as the setting of the daily ritual of *salutatio*, the paying of respects by clients to their powerful patrons.

In the larger houses, where space was not at a premium, the *atrium* was surrounded by a full panoply of rooms, and there was frequently a peristyle (or even two) and further ranges of rooms at the rear. We have commented on the social structuring of such mansions in earlier chapters. Whereas the front part, focusing on the *atrium*, was reserved for more formal reception, the peristyle complex was where the owner received and entertained a closer circle of friends and associates. But even in the inner quarters the house was never truly 'private' in the sense that we understand today. People came and went in a manner that to us would seem astonishing. This situation is bound up with the very nature of the Pompeian household.[34] Rather than a household in the modern sense, this has been aptly dubbed a 'houseful': in addition to the owner and his immediate family and slaves, there would have been what Wallace-Hadrill describes as a 'fluctuating assortment of dependents, freedmen, workers, friends and lodgers'. The numbers of people in residence at any given time would have varied but was normally substantial.

The size of the house's population helps to explain the number of rooms. Some houses had 20, 30, 40 or even more rooms on the ground floor, and there were often, in addition, upstairs apartments whose extent and arrangement are unknown. One of the incentives to the insertion of upper storeys may, indeed, have been the proliferation of dependent relatives and other hangers-on. But not all rooms were in constant use. One phenomenon that has often been noted is the duplication of dining rooms and reception rooms. If we can believe the ancient writers, they could have been reserved for different times of the year: winter dining rooms faced south-west to take advantage of the afternoon sun, while dining rooms for spring and autumn faced east, and summer ones north, to achieve appropriate temperatures in the hotter seasons. Alternatively, the householder could have switched from one room to another according to the size of a dinner party or the social standing of his guests; or he may simply have wanted to vary the setting. The different dining rooms had different colour schemes and different pictorial themes. When the Roman magnate Lucullus told his servants, in a story recounted by Plutarch,[35] that he would entertain a pair of especially honoured guests in his 'Apollo', he was choosing a dining room appropriate to the occasion, one which was probably decorated with pictures relevant to that deity. This episode took place in Rome, but similar choices were certainly available in the big houses of Pompeii.

As a corollary to varying patterns of room-use, it seems that rooms were not kept fully furnished. There are grounds for believing that items such as chairs, dining couches and tables were shifted from one room to another as occasion demanded.[36] Generally speaking, archaeological finds reveal a much lower level of furnishing than we are accustomed to nowadays, and some rooms may have remained unfurnished when not in use. This has the further consequence that rooms may have been multi-functional. Even where patterns of floor or wall decoration indicate the position of a bed or of dining couches, it is dangerous to infer that the rooms in question invariably functioned as bedrooms or dining rooms. A room in the House of the Craftsman (I.10.7) whose pavement marks out the standard pi-shaped arrangement of couches in a *triclinium* and would thus imply that it was intended for dining actually contained only a single couch at the time of the eruption, which would suggest that it was then serving as a bedroom. But even the presence of a single couch does not necessarily entitle us to think of any chamber as a bedroom *tout court*. The Latin word *cubiculum*, frequently translated as 'bedroom', is shown from literary sources to have comprised not only rooms in which people slept but also rooms for daytime rest, study or intimate meetings between friends. Conversely, not all residents in a house would have slept on beds or even in designated rooms. Slaves, in particular, may have had mattresses on the floor, stationed at the door of the master's bedroom or in various other parts of the house. Arrangements were flexible in the extreme.

The *atrium* house was not the only kind of dwelling in the city. Another type was the so-called 'Hoffmann house' (*14*) in which the place of an *atrium* was taken by a cross-hall (or open court?). There were also many small units of no more than two or three rooms. Numerous commercial establishments fit into this last category, in that they consisted merely of a shop or workshop with one or two living rooms at the rear or alternatively with a mezzanine reached by an internal ladder or stairway. Other dwellings were situated entirely on an upper floor, being self-contained flats reached either from within a house or via a stairway opening directly from the street (*64*).

Details of ownership and tenancy arrangements, doubtless as complex and varied as in most modern cities, are largely lost to us. According to Roman law, the ownership of any upper floor remained vested in the proprietor of the ground floor, so the residents of upstairs apartments were presumably tenants or family dependents of whoever owned the house or other premises over which they lived. Similarly, one can assume that many shops or small dwelling units clustered along the periphery of grand *atrium* houses were the property of the main householder who rented them out to their various occupiers. Some confirmation of Pompeian practice in this respect is afforded by a couple of advertisements that have survived in the form of painted notices on street walls.[37] The first, thought to relate to *insula* VI.6, runs: 'Insula Arriana Polliana owned by Cn. Alleius Nigidius Maius: to rent, from 1 July next, shops with their own mezzanines, respectable upstairs apartments, and a house [or houses]. Prospective tenants should apply to Primus, Cn. Alleius Nigidius Maius' slave.' This *insula* had probably once belonged to Arrius Pollio, but by AD 79 had come into the possession of Cn. Alleius Nigidius Maius, one of the city's leading figures, who may have resided in the dominant central house, the so-called House of Pansa. The second advertisement, found on the wall of II.2, offers a bath-suite, shops, mezzanines, and upstairs apartments in the *Praedia* of Julia Felix; here the leases were to run for five years from 13 August. In each case it appears that the whole *insula* was owned by a single proprietor who capitalised on his or her

assets by letting a number of the outlying units. But this does not mean that the same situation obtained in every *insula*. In most cases, irregular patterns of division within a block, coupled with signs of independent planning in different dwellings, strongly suggest that there was no single proprietor but rather a number of separate owner-occupiers.

One last matter for comment is the nature of interior decoration. Extraordinary care was lavished upon the adornment of floors, walls and ceilings. Where the modern world is content with linoleum, carpets, patterned wallpaper etc., the Pompeians – like the inhabitants of all romanised cities of the late Republic and early Empire – aspired to individually crafted decorations of some artistic pretension. Pavements received patterns of coloured stones or tesserae set in mortar, or in some cases geometric or figured mosaics (*19, 30, colour plate 4*); walls were embellished with painted schemes carried out on fresh plaster in the fresco technique (*colour plates 1, 3, 6, 10, 12, 15, 31*); ceilings were again painted in fresco, or alternatively worked in stucco relief. This extravagance seems, at least by the city's last period, to have permeated all levels of society. Obviously not every room was decorated in an ambitious manner. Even in the great mansions, where large areas of floor surface had mosaic paving and all the principal living and reception spaces had walls painted with polychrome compositions articulated with architectural elements and containing mythological pictures (*colour plates 13, 16*), landscapes, still lifes, and the like – compositions assignable to the so-called Pompeian Styles – there were many minor rooms with much simpler decorations, such as plain mortar pavements or white-ground wall-paintings divided into simple panels by painted bands and lines. In the poorer houses the more pretentious paintings were limited to a main reception room and perhaps a privileged bedroom, but no more. But what is significant is that every householder wanted such decorations.

There were, of course, wide variations in quality: the finest work is found in the grander houses, and some of the paintings in the smaller houses (and in less favoured rooms in the wealthy ones) are poorly done, if not slapdash. Such differences must have reflected differences of cost: the better artists were able to charge more than the average jobbing craftsmen. Even within good quality work there was evidently a sliding scale of fees corresponding to the ambition of a scheme: elaborate polychrome paintings featuring mythological pictures cost the most, and simpler compositions with landscapes, still life panels or animal vignettes, carried out in a more restricted range of colours, came below. Yet all such decorations involved a considerable outlay, and the time required to produce them would have caused major disruptions to daily life. The fact that the social imperatives constrained householders to undergo such disruptions speaks volumes. There has been no other society in the history of the western world that has gone to such lengths to beautify domestic interiors.

64 Street entrance (VIII.3.10) with a stairway leading directly to an upstairs flat. *Photograph R.J. Ling* 113/33

THE URBAN FABRIC

The effects of the earthquake or earthquakes preceding the eruption meant that Pompeii was functioning anything but normally in AD 79. The temple of the city's patron goddess Venus was evidently out of commission, countless houses were undergoing repair and reconstruction, and even the water supply seems not to have been fully operational. In these circumstances, to review the urban fabric – the ways in which patterns of building, the street system, the water supply and the provision of drainage structured life in the city – involves recreating an ideal scenario, such as might have been obtained if the disaster of AD 62 had never occurred.

Firstly, the distribution of buildings within the city.[38] Here an unusual feature is the concentration of civic and religious buildings in the south-west quarter. This phenomenon, as we have seen, resulted from the topography and history of the site: the original nucleus, with its central forum, seems to have been laid out on the crest of the escarpment commanding the coast road and river mouth, and this remained the focus of public life even after the settlement expanded to the north and east. Other major public buildings were located elsewhere because of specific needs. The large and small theatres took advantage of the natural declivity in the central southern sector; the amphitheatre was sited to exploit the pre-existing bank of earth inside the eastern corner of the defences and to marginalise the large crowds which would be attracted to the city on the days of the games. The Campus was placed adjacent to the amphitheatre probably because this was the best location to secure a large expanse of relatively flat ground in an area which was not heavily built up, so would not entail excessive costs in expropriation. The public baths were positioned to benefit the maximum numbers of citizens. The earliest, the Stabian Baths, situated at the pivotal junction of Via dell'Abbondanza and Via Stabiana, served the southern and eastern parts of the city; the Forum Baths, immediately to the north of the forum, serviced the north-west quarter; and the Central Baths, at the junction of Via Stabiana and Via di Nola, would (when complete) have catered for those in the north and north-eastern regions. The Suburban Baths, outside the Marine Gate, may have been intended for dwellers in the port and riverside suburbs.

Of other types of buildings, shops and workshops were, not surprisingly, heavily concentrated along the main thoroughfares, especially Via dell'Abbondanza, Via Stabiana, and the northern *decumanus* represented by Via delle Terme, Via della Fortuna and Via di Nola. There were no permanent shops opening directly onto the forum (though graffiti and pictorial representations indicate that temporary stalls were set up against the surrounding porticoes), but this was more than compensated for by the presence of a veritable shopping district immediately to the north, where purpose-built units ran along the street façades of the Macellum and the Forum Baths. Further shops lined Via degli Augustali, which struck off eastwards from this commercial quarter, and there was another cluster along Via dei Teatri, the street which led from Via dell'Abbondanza to the Triangular Forum and the theatre quarter. All the streets in question were routes which would have received considerable volumes of pedestrian traffic. As in modern cities, retail outlets naturally gravitated to the places where they were most likely to attract customers.

The remaining areas of the city were occupied by housing. While the unexcavated parts in the east are, of course, unknown quantities, there is nothing along their periphery to suggest that they contained further important public buildings or industrial complexes. This means that six of the nine regions (I, III, IV, V, VI and IX) were dedicated overwhelmingly to residential accommodation. There were also large numbers of houses in Regions VII and VIII, around and between the two aggregations of public buildings in the forum and theatre quarters. Only Region II, much of which was swallowed up by the Campus and amphitheatre, had more limited space for habitation.

Within the residential areas there were some broad differences. The density of building was sparser in the easternmost quarters, Regions I-III, where many early houses had given way to vineyards and gardens during the city's later years. In the old quarter to the east of the forum, there was a comparatively high proportion of modest houses and workshops as opposed to luxurious mansions. The latter were concentrated chiefly in Region VI and immediately to the east of Via Stabiana, i.e. in the western parts of Regions I, IX and V, while a further swathe of desirable residences ran along the western and southern fringes of the city, spilling in terraces over the old defensive walls. But it would be wrong to think of poor 'inner-city' districts and affluent neighbourhoods further from the centre. There was none of the zoning to which we are accustomed in modern cities. The 'old city' contained many relatively big and well-appointed houses, while small and unpretentious dwellings were ubiquitous in the outlying zones. What is striking about Pompeii, and about other cities of the ancient Mediterranean that are sufficiently well preserved for patterns of habitation to be discerned, is the way that members of the elite lived cheek-by-jowl with their poorer neighbours. Time and again we find *insulae* dominated by a single wealthy residence, complete with lofty *atrium* (or *atria*), spacious peristyle, and sumptuous wall-paintings, but containing also small houses, shops, workshops, and one- or two-room apartments – some of them, as we have seen, occupied by tenants of the main proprietor. This was not a rare situation; it was absolutely normal.

Secondly, the streets. Streets were, of course, vital to the functioning of the city, being the essential means of communication between one district and another, as well as between the intramural area and the suburbs. They handled both wheeled traffic and pedestrians (65). For the former, mainly carts and wagons drawn by pack-animals, there were carriageways paved with polygonal blocks of basalt, carefully fitted to form a solid and durable (if very bumpy) surface; for the latter there were raised sidewalks, surfaced with pebbles, mortar, or compacted earth. The paving of the sidewalks was apparently the responsibility of individual householders, since it often changes from one property to the

65 Detail of a Pompeian roadway (Via dell'Abbondanza) showing stepping stones for pedestrians and the ruts which enabled wheeled vehicles to negotiate a course between them. *Photograph R.J. Ling 112/14*

next, but the roadways were certainly maintained by the civic authorities. The process of paving the streets seems to have been long drawn out: while some of the stones show carved letters that may imply a date in the late Republic, most of the side streets in Regions I and II (if not also in the unexcavated regions) were still unsurfaced in 79. Even where streets were paved, it is clear that they were frequently deep in mire, and for the convenience of pedestrians there were regular crossing points formed by stepping stones.

The relative importance of streets and the volume of traffic that they carried can be inferred from their width. The principal thoroughfares, such as Via dell'Abbondanza, Via Stabiana and Via di Nola, which in places measure 8.50m (28ft), were double the width of many of the side streets, and some other routes, notably Via del Foro and Via del Tempio d'Iside, were even wider (up to 9.50m). But not all streets were accessible to wheeled vehicles: movement was regulated by barriers of various kinds.[39] The street along the east side of the House of the Labyrinth, for example, was closed by a bollard at the south end, there were barricades blocking access to most of the side streets opening off the south side of Via dell'Abbondanza, and, following encroachment by the rear wall of the Central Baths, the street between *insulae* IX.4 and 5 became too narrow to admit vehicles. More surprisingly, the western stretch of Via dell'Abbondanza was accessible neither from the west, where the forum was a pedestrian zone, nor from the east, where the intersection with Via Stabiana was marked by a step in level (50cm) that no vehicle could have negotiated; the only means of entry was from Vico di Eumachia on the north side and from Via dei Teatri on the south. These and other patterns of traffic flow can be read from the remains of ruts worn (or cut) in the paving of the carriageways. How far the visible arrangements reflect a coherent policy on the part of the authorities is a matter for debate; but in certain cases there are clear signs that measures were taken to close routes which had previously been open, or alternatively to force drivers over to one side of a road to avoid collisions with incoming vehicles at junctions. The whole question of the working and regulation of Pompeii's traffic movement is one that merits further study.

Thirdly, water supply and drainage.[40] By the final years Pompeii had become accustomed to running water, brought to the city via a branch of the aqueduct which ran from Serino, in the hills east of Avellino, to Naples and Puteoli. Water arrived first at the *castellum aquae* (66), a roofed reservoir situated at the highest point of the city, next to the Vesuvius Gate, where it was filtered by bronze grilles and a sediment trap before issuing through three ducts in the south wall. It has often been claimed, on the basis of a passage in Vitruvius, that one of the outlets served the public fountains, a second the baths and other public buildings, and the third the private houses; the supply to one or the other could then have been adjusted or turned off if, for any reason, there was a need to cut consumption. But to have run three parallel systems of this type through much of the city would have been enormously complicated and hardly viable: it is much more likely that the division was regional, with three mains leading to different parts of the city.

The water was distributed entirely by the force of gravity. From the Castellum Aquae, approximately 42.50m (140ft) above modern sea level, there was a fall of 35m (115ft) to the city's lowest point, at the Stabiae Gate, and falls of 15-30m to the south-eastern and south-western margins. This was more than adequate to ensure a steady flow. Heavy lead pipes with an internal diameter of 15 or 16.5cm (6 or 6.5in) and walls 1.5cm (0.5in) thick carried the water under the sidewalks, emerging at intervals to rise to the top of towers which controlled the pressure and sent it forward via small-gauge pipes to service their immediate neighbourhoods. These towers, of which there are at least 14 known, form one of the distinctive features of the urban landscape (30). Up to 6m (20ft) high and built of small blocks of tuff, they contain vertical slots in the sides to accommodate the upflow and downflow pipes, while at the top was a header tank of lead 65cm (2ft 2in) square and 56cm (1ft 10in) deep.

The prime purpose of the water supply was to keep the public fountains running.[41] Situated mostly at street corners, where they were easily accessible to nearby residents, these consisted of square basins, generally made of slabs of

66 Castellum Aquae (water distributor) inside the Vesuvius Gate, viewed from the south-east. Three holes at the foot of the south wall contained the pipes through which the water issued to the city. *Photograph J.B. Ward-Perkins*

lava, with a pillar on one side containing a spout from which the water flowed. The pillars are decorated with carved emblems, including the cock (7) and the figure of Abundantia (67) on which modern street names have been based. In all, we know of 40 examples, and can extrapolate at least another half dozen in the unexcavated areas. For most householders there was a fountain within 50m (165ft) of their front doors; only in the more sparsely populated quarters, notably in the eastern part of the city, was the distribution less regular.

After the fountains the most important recipients of water were the public buildings. Especially demanding were the baths. Here, ample reservoir tanks offered an emergency 'fall-back' in the event of disruptions to the aqueduct supply. That on the roof of the Stabian Baths, a survivor from the period when water was winched up from an adjacent well, is thought to have been able to hold 38,500 litres (nearly 8,500 gallons). The one which served the Forum Baths, located across the street to the west, is calculated to have had a capacity of 430,000 litres (nearly 95,000 gallons).

67 Street fountain decorated with a relief of Abundantia (Abundance), which gives its name to the main street Via dell'Abbondanza. *Photograph L.A. Ling*

In comparison with these public needs, householders would have had low priority. Several houses used running water in garden features, especially fountain niches or water-pouring statues, and in some cases these features were extravagant in their consumption: the garden of the House of the Vettii, for example, boasted 14 jets, while those of Julia Felix and D. Octavius Quartio contained elaborate fountain pavilions and long canals (*31*). But the majority of dwellings were not connected to the mains. The expense of paying the local water rates, the existence of which is confirmed by Vitruvius and Frontinus (who wrote a treatise on the water system of Rome),[42] no doubt acted as a disincentive, because such houses evidently continued to rely for most of their requirements upon the traditional method of collecting rainwater in underground cisterns.

The provision of running water was one of the most important aspects of the functioning of the city. It involved a technological sophistication unmatched by other services, and presumably cost considerable sums in materials (lead pipes, tanks and distribution boxes, bronze taps, stopcocks, filters etc.) and maintenance. The scale of the operation can be gauged from some statistics. It has been conjectured that the daily flow of water into the city was in the order of 6,480,000 litres (1,425,430 gallons). The network of pipes required to distribute this water to its various destinations – not counting the length of the aqueduct outside the walls – must have extended to several kilometres. Keeping the system in order and regulating the supply certainly represented a major burden for the local administration.

The final element to be considered is drainage. Surplus water from the fountains, public buildings and houses had to be disposed of; in addition, as many visitors to modern Pompeii will know all too well, the city is prone to torrential storms, and there had to be measures to deal with the rain. The answer was to use the streets. The overflow of the fountains ran into the roadways, and from houses and other buildings such rainwater as could not be accommodated within the cisterns was channelled via underground drains to discharge through holes in the kerbs. Since the majority of the streets sloped steeply, the gradient carried the water away, helping in the process to cleanse the roadways of the filth that tended to accumulate within them. Ultimately the water was collected in storm drains or sewers, which transported it to the exterior of the city. Entrances to such sewers can be found at certain strategic places – at the junction of Via dell'Abbondanza and Via Stabiana, for instance, and at the points where roads (Via delle Scuole and Via Marina) issue from the south and west of the forum.

Rainwater was exploited also to flush latrines. Within houses, this was often managed with the aid of downpipes, formed of terracotta tubes or of cylindrical amphorae fitted into one another, which brought water directly from the roofs. The sewage from latrines, however, was not normally transmitted into the main drains but debouched into deep cesspits under the streets. A series of four of these has been discovered in recent excavations in an alleyway to the east of *insula* IX.12; they were apparently in the process of being cleaned out at the time of the eruption.[43]

SUMMARY

Pompeii informs us, therefore, about civic administration, religious practice, economic activity, entertainments and domestic life within a small south Italian city of the early Roman Empire. It also reveals something of how the city functioned in terms of the distribution of different kinds of buildings, the operation of its street system, the provision of running water, and the disposal of rainwater and other waste. In addition to all this, there is much that we can learn from the bric-à-brac and graffiti found in the excavations – material that we have barely touched upon. Gold jewellery reveals how Pompeians liked to adorn themselves, glassware and metal vessels indicate the trappings of the dinner table (*colour plates 28* and *29*), bone and ivory gaming pieces testify to the playing of board games (*colour plate 30*), graffiti tell us about amorous encounters, quarrels, the price of commodities – one could continue indefinitely. Pompeii is an inexhaustible fund of knowledge about life in Roman times. We must now turn, however, from a description of the world that was abruptly destroyed in the cataclysm of AD 79 to recount the story of its rediscovery and excavation.

7

POMPEII AFTER THE ERUPTION

The destruction of Pompeii and Herculaneum was the worst natural disaster ever to have affected the Roman world, and it left a deep impression. Later Roman writers frequently refer to it. A hundred years after the event, for example, the philosopher-emperor Marcus Aurelius cites the end of the two cities as an example of the transience of things.[1]

In the immediate aftermath of the eruption there was clearly relief work to be undertaken. The emperor Titus is known to have been in Campania in AD 80 to inspect the situation. According to literary sources, he appointed a pair of ex-consuls, chosen by lot, to act as commissioners for the restoration of the region, and allowed them to dedicate the property of any victims without surviving heirs towards the repair of the affected cities. He himself also gave financial help.

One must imagine that much of the relief went to cities on the periphery of the devastated area, which were damaged but not wiped out, and which would have had to cope with an influx of refugees (a quarter in Naples was named after people who had escaped from Herculaneum). For the buried cities themselves there was no hope of exhumation; the best that could be accomplished was the retrieval of property and materials. Herculaneum of course was too deeply buried to be accessible. At Pompeii, however, the upper parts of higher buildings would still have been visible above the mantle of ash, and it must have been easy to trace the street plan and locate open spaces such as the forum, so the survivors could have targeted places to dig. There is clear evidence throughout the city of the salvaging or plunder of marbles, metals, artworks and other items of value. All of the statues of the forum are missing, and it is difficult to believe, as has been suggested, that they had been put in some store pending restoration that was in progress in 79: it is much more likely that they were retrieved in order to recycle the valuable bronze. Similarly, all the cult statues of Pompeii's temples (apart from a couple of fragments in the Capitolium and terracotta statues in the temple of Aesculapius) seem to have been removed. Even some of the limestone paving slabs of the forum and the marble veneer of surrounding buildings are missing, and once again the likely explanation is that they were salvaged for use elsewhere, not that they were awaiting installation in an unfinished refurbishment.

Countless houses and other buildings at Pompeii are riddled with holes dug by later tunnellers in search of booty (*68*). In some cases the presence of datable

68 Holes made by tunnellers in the House of the Lovers (I.10.11). By digging through the walls the plunderers avoided the loose material in open spaces. *Photograph J.B. Ward-Perkins*

objects belonging to the second, third or fourth centuries AD confirms that such disturbance continued long after the eruption. There is even evidence of intrusion in the early Christian and medieval periods. The result of such disruptive activity is to reduce the archaeological usefulness of studying the distribution of finds (already complicated by the effects of the earthquake and dislocation during the eruption itself). Many objects were removed from the ruins altogether, while others were shifted from one place to another and thus divorced from their original contexts. This problem is particularly acute in closed rooms, because it was precisely these spaces, which had not been filled with pumice and ashes – thus permitting diggers to operate under the shelter of roofs and ceilings without the risk of being buried by landslides – that were most extensively ransacked. Open spaces, such as *atria* and gardens, where the volcanic deposits were deep and unstable, have largely escaped the depredations.

In the Middle Ages, as the volcanic deposits gradually weathered to become cultivable soil and the visible masonry was robbed for building materials, the site of Pompeii disappeared under olive groves and vineyards, and knowledge of the buried city became little more than a folk memory perpetuated by the name of the locality: 'la Città' ('the city'). The first major event in its rediscovery was the digging, between 1592 and 1600, of a channel for an aqueduct to carry water from the River Sarno to armaments factories at Torre Annunziata; this aqueduct, designed by the architect Domenico Fontana, followed the contours of the volcanic spurs to the south of Vesuvius, except at the hill of Città, where it went deep underground, cutting through a series of ancient houses. But, even though the finds included coins and inscriptions, it was not generally recognised that Fontana had stumbled on the remains of the lost city.

This discovery was the first of several. In 1689 an excavation in search of water yielded further inscriptions, one of which apparently included a specific reference to Pompeii. A contemporary historian correctly divined that Città was the site of Pompeii and, though others were sceptical, the same view was taken by Giuseppe Macrini, who in 1693 reported having himself seen well-preserved remains of buried buildings.[2]

The real breakthrough in the re-emergence of the buried cities came not at the relatively accessible site of Pompeii but at the deeply buried Herculaneum. Here, in 1709, a smallholder digging a shaft for a well chanced upon an ancient building adorned with white and coloured marbles. News of this discovery came to the attention of the Prince d'Elbeuf, a cavalry officer in the service of the Austrian imperial army which had just taken over Naples and southern Italy; he promptly bought the smallholder's land and instituted excavations for material to decorate a villa that he was planning to build. In a campaign lasting seven years, conducted by means of tunnels radiating from the original well, d'Elbeuf unearthed spectacular remains of architectural elements and sculptures, notably three marble statues of draped females which he smuggled out of Italy as a gift to his patron, Prince Eugene of Savoy, in Vienna (they eventually ended up in Dresden).

Shortly after this, the kingdom of Naples passed into the hands of Philip V of Spain who vested it in his eldest son Charles of Bourbon. The new king learnt of the discoveries of d'Elbeuf and in 1738 resumed explorations at the site of the well, entrusting their supervision to a Spanish engineer, Rocque Joachin de Alcubierre. There was almost immediately a notable success when the finding of fragments of an inscription revealed that the building under investigation was a theatre; and it was not long before further inscriptions established that it was the theatre of Herculaneum.[3] Excavations were now pursued with renewed vigour. The theatre yielded more exciting discoveries, including equestrian statues of bronze. More spectacular still were the discoveries at a new site in the vicinity, a luxurious villa replete with bronze and marble sculptures (69), which became known as the Villa of the Papyri after the library of scrolls found there in 1752.

The excavations at Herculaneum were expensive and laborious because of the depth at which they lay and the hardness of the volcanic material in which they were encased. Lack of light, the risk of roof falls in the tunnels, the potential danger of asphyxiation from noxious gases – all contributed to the difficulty of the enterprise. As a result, in 1748 the king authorised the start of work at Cività, where walls and chance finds had continued to turn up. The excavators soon found painted walls, as well as the first skeleton of a victim, accompanied by gold and silver coins. Further excavations, sunk here and there almost at random, came down on the amphitheatre and the so-called Villa of Cicero outside the Herculaneum Gate, while from 1755 to 1757 there was a major campaign in the *Praedia* of Julia Felix. But it was not at first accepted by everyone that the site at Cività was Pompeii (Alcubierre insisted on identifying it as Stabiae). The turning point came in 1763, when an investigation immediately outside the Herculaneum Gate produced a stone block with the inscription recording T. Suedius Clemens' commission to restore illegally occupied land 'to the community of Pompeii' (*rei publicae Pompeianorum*).[4] From now on there could be no doubt that Cività was Pompeii.

Attention shifted definitively from Herculaneum, where work was abandoned in 1765, to the more amenable site of Pompeii. Here, for the first time, the volcanic deposits were fully removed from buildings under excavation, and the ancient remains permanently exposed to view. Under a new king, Ferdinand IV, who acceded to the throne as a minor in 1759 and who left all archaeological matters in the hands of his chief minister Bernardo Tanucci, a succession of buildings was brought to light – in 1764 the temple of Isis (70), in 1765 the large theatre and the Triangular Forum, in 1771 the so-called Villa of Diomedes in the Street of the Tombs, where the finding of 20 bodies huddled in a cryptoportico created something of a sensation.

The excavation of Pompeii was now firmly underway. But the techniques adopted by the early excavators left much to be desired. The overwhelming motivation of the work was the search for treasures, especially objects of gold and silver, and works of art. Paintings were cut from walls to be taken to

69 Bronze bust from the Villa of the Papyri at Herculaneum, possibly based on a portrait of the Hellenistic king Seleucus I (died 281 BC). Ht 55cm. Naples Museum 5590. *Photograph Getty Research Library, Wim Swaan collection 96.P.21*

70 Excavation of the temple of Isis: hand-coloured engraving in Sir William Hamilton's *Campi Phlegraei. Observations on the Volcanoes of the Two Sicilies* (1776), pl. XLI

embellish the royal palace at Portici near Herculaneum (and after 1779 to the palace in Naples which subsequently became the National Museum), and the ancient buildings were treated with scant regard, being left to the mercy of the elements without protection or consolidation. Any paintings that were surplus to requirements were often deliberately smashed to prevent them fuelling a black market. The siting of the trenches reflected the nature of the enterprise. The diggers moved from one area to another, abandoning each site as soon as they decided that its riches had been exhausted and that there was no point in continuing the investigation. Amid this chaos, special commendation has to be reserved for the Swiss engineer Karl Weber, Alcubierre's assistant from 1750 to 1764, who drew meticulous plans of the subterranean excavations at Herculaneum – no small feat given the difficulties of surveying buildings known only from a network of tunnels – as well as of the *Praedia* of Julia Felix at Pompeii (71) and of a complex of villas that had come to light at Stabiae. Accompanying inventories of statues and other significant discoveries, with keys to the find-spots, provide invaluable assistance to the modern

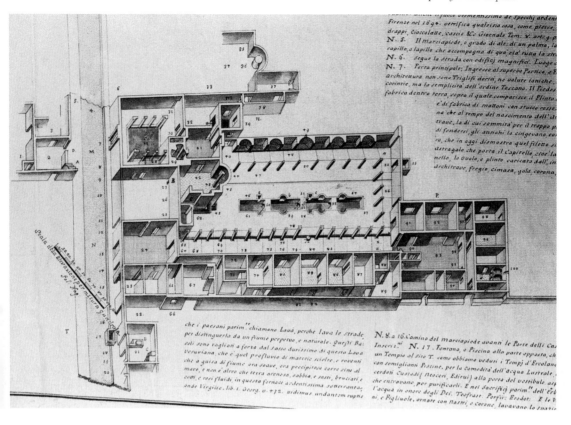

71 Axonometric reconstruction drawing of the *Praedia* of Julia Felix (II.4.3) drawn by Karl Weber. *Photograph C.C. Parslow (courtesy of Archaeological Superintendency Naples)*

archaeologists who have re-examined the sites. Weber's example served to inspire his successor Francesco La Vega, who prepared the first general plans of Pompeii and Herculaneum (as then known).

For much of the early Bourbon period, knowledge of the excavations was jealously guarded against outsiders. Several visitors from northern and western Europe came to Naples as part of the Grand Tour but, unless they had an *entrée* to the royal court, they were not allowed to see the discoveries. If admitted to the museum or the excavations, it was under close supervision. Even J.J. Winckelmann, the greatest living student of ancient art, was granted only restricted visits and was forbidden from taking notes or making sketches. His reports on the excavations and finds, which played an important part in bringing them to the world's attention, had to be written from memory. The Bourbon court – like many subsequent excavators across the ages – reserved publication rights for themselves. The eventual outcome was a set of seven lavish tomes of engravings entitled *Le Antichità di Ercolano*, published between 1757 and 1779 under the aegis of the Real Accademia Ercolanese di Archeologia (Royal

Herculaneum Academy of Archaeology). It was symptomatic of the time that these volumes concentrated almost exclusively on paintings, statuary and bronze objects, which were considered in isolation and subjected to highly learned but largely arid discourses.

The *Antichità* brought knowledge of the discoveries in the buried cities to a wider public, and encouraged a new wave of tourists. In 1787 the German poet Goethe paid a first visit to Pompeii, accompanied by the painters Tischbein and Hackert. His memorable judgement was, 'There have been many disasters in the world, but few that have given so much pleasure to posterity.'[5] In the meantime excavations were carried along the road that entered the city via the Herculaneum Gate, and La Vega uncovered two of the archetypal *atrium* houses, those of the Surgeon and of Sallust. But events in France soon overshadowed the archaeological programme. The French Revolution of 1789 instilled fear in the monarchies of Europe, not least that of Naples, and during the following decade the conquests of Napoleon turned fear to reality.

After a first temporary occupation in 1798-99, France took over the kingdom of Naples in 1805, forcing Ferdinand IV into exile in Sicily. Under French rule, the excavation of Pompeii, which had slowed down in recent years, was pursued with unprecedented zeal. The new king, Napoleon's brother Joseph Bonaparte, picked up a project of La Vega to join together the 'islands' of excavation in the west of the city to form a continuous tract. This objective was finally achieved by Joseph's successors, his sister Caroline and her consort Joachim Murat, who took over in 1808 and set to work with even greater energy, elevating the excavations to a major state activity and lavishing large sums of money on them. They directed their efforts to exposing the city walls, and, from 1812 onwards, the forum and its surrounding buildings. At the same time, Queen Caroline's support of the French architect Charles François Mazois led to the production of *Les ruines de Pompéi*, a four-volume compendium of measured drawings and descriptions of the buildings excavated in this period, which remains, even now, a landmark in the recording of the ancient city.

After the restoration of the Bourbons in 1814, there was a certain loss of momentum, as the returning Ferdinand was unwilling or unable to invest so heavily in the excavations. Nonetheless, important finds continued to be made, notably the Forum Baths in 1824, the House of the Tragic Poet, with its wonderful series of mythological figure paintings, still in 1824 and, most spectacular of all, in 1830-32, the vast House of the Faun, resplendent with First Style wall-decorations and figured mosaics, including the remarkable Alexander Mosaic.

In this second Bourbon period there was a spate of publications which brought information about the discoveries at Pompeii to the outside world. Most ambitious were the 16 volumes of *Real Museo Borbonico* (1824-57), containing engravings of the items in Naples Museum, and the collections of coloured lithographs prepared by Wilhelm Zahn (*colour plate 31*), Wilhelm Ternite and, beginning in 1854, the brothers Fausto and Felice Niccolini. But there were also

72 Music performance in the Pompeian house of Prince Jérôme Napoleon in Paris. Painting by G. Boulanger (1861), now in Versailles. *Photograph University of Manchester, Art History collection*

more popular accounts, such as William Gell's *Pompeiana*, first published in 1817-19, which went through numerous editions and was updated by a supplement in 1832. This did much to popularise Pompeii in Britain, and directly influenced Edward Bulwer Lytton, who produced his famous novel *The Last Days of Pompeii* in 1834. At the same time the discoveries created a fashion for modern houses decorated in the Pompeian style, the best known of which were one based on the House of the Dioscuri built by Ludwig I of Bavaria at Aschaffenburg in the 1840s, and the house of Prince Jérôme Napoleon in the Avenue Montaigne in Paris (1854-59) (*72*).

The fame of Pompeii now brought many visitors. Among the distinguished literary figures to make the trip were Shelley, who recorded his impressions in an *Ode to Naples*, Sir Walter Scott, who was carried round in a sedan chair with Gell as a *cicerone* shortly before he died, and Charles Dickens, the highlight of whose visit was not the buried city but the ascent of Vesuvius. There was also a regular stream of heads of state for whose benefit, in continuation of a practice which had begun already in the previous century, exciting discoveries were specially stage-managed.

A new chapter in the history of the excavations came with the unification of Italy in 1860. After a brief interlude in which the directorship was entrusted to

Alexandre Dumas the novelist – whose main achievement was to systematise and catalogue the *gabinetto segreto* (the collection of phallic objects and erotic paintings) in the Naples museum – responsibility for continuing the work passed to the archaeologist and numismatist Giuseppe Fiorelli, who had at one stage been imprisoned by the Bourbons for his involvement with a revolutionary faction. Fiorelli had started a history of the excavations (*Pompeianarum Antiquitatum Historia*) while in prison and brought to his new position a fresh purpose and new ideas. He launched a systematic programme of joining up the areas left between previous excavations, especially in the north-west quarter, and he reversed (where possible) the policy of removing paintings and other artworks to Naples Museum, preferring to leave them in their contexts so that visitors could appreciate the site itself as a museum. For movable objects, however, he created a small antiquarium in the excavations. But his two most long-lasting contributions were to institute the system of postal addresses, with numbered regions, *insulae* and doorways, that we still use today, and to devise the technique of taking plaster casts of the voids

73 Cast of a dead Pompeian, obtained using the technique pioneered by G. Fiorelli in 1863. *Photograph Ward-Perkins collection*

left by rotted human bodies (73). This second contribution, later extended to the recovery of tree trunks and wooden objects (wheels, doors (47), window-shutters and furniture), brought to life the drama of the city's destruction and the human tragedy that it represented in a way that no number of houses, wall-decorations and artefacts seen in isolation could ever have done. The 'petrified' corpses have justly become a grim and intensely evocative tourist attraction.

The new systematic methods introduced by Fiorelli paved the way for scholarly syntheses of the material revealed by the excavations. In 1868 Wolfgang Helbig published his catalogue of figure paintings, arranged by themes.[6] In 1871 Karl Zangemeister edited the first instalment of *Corpus Inscriptionum Latinarum* iv, devoted to the graffiti and dipinti on the walls of Pompeii and the other buried cities. Most important was August Mau's classification of the four Pompeian 'styles' of wall-decoration, adumbrated in an article that came out in 1873, and fully expounded in his monumental *Geschichte der decorativen Wandmalerei in Pompeji*, published in 1882. This study, based on meticulous analysis of the paintings themselves and their archaeological context, as well as comparative data from buildings in Rome and clues in ancient writers, notably Vitruvius, succeeded in imposing order on what had previously been an amorphous mass of material. It provided an essential typological and chronological framework which remains as valid today as it was 120 years ago.

Fiorelli's successors Michele Ruggiero, Giulio De Petra, Ettore Pais and Antonio Sogliano continued excavating the residential quarters of the city. Among the houses uncovered in this period were that of the Vettii (1894-95) and that of the Gilded Cupids (1902-05), both of which were restored to become showpieces with their marble and bronze furnishings and sculptures displayed in (imaginatively) replanted gardens (74). The attempt to recreate such garden ensembles represented a further important step in the conversion of the excavated houses into museums of ancient life, and it is sad that the modern age has forced a change of policy, the theft of five bronze statuettes from the Vettii garden in 1978 having led to the original works being removed into store.

In 1910 the appointment of Vittorio Spinazzola, with a vastly increased budget, opened a new phase of large-scale exploration. Spinazzola launched a major campaign aimed at clearing Via dell'Abbondanza to link the excavations in the western half of the city with the amphitheatre. The outstanding contribution of this campaign was to recover the house and shop façades of a busy commercial street, not just at ground level but also on upper floors. Following and developing techniques established by Fiorelli, Spinazzola's excavations descended level by level from the top of the volcanic deposits rather than cutting into them from the side as one might a quarry face; this permitted a better understanding of the processes of Pompeii's burial and destruction but, more important, it enabled the upper parts of buildings to be salvaged. Where the earlier method had inevitably provoked the collapse of upper storeys, they were now recorded, restored and consolidated before the lower ones were uncovered: restoration proceeded *pari*

74 Garden of the House of the Vettii (VI.15.1) as reconstructed after the excavations of 1894-95 and before the thefts of 1978. *Photograph University of Manchester, Art History collection*

passu with excavation. As a result, it was possible for the first time in the history of Pompeii's excavations to reproduce something of the appearance of one of the main streets, complete with upstairs loggias, jetties and pent roofs. Spinazzola also excavated several complete houses opening from the street, notably the House of the Cryptoportico and the House of D. Octavius Quartio. In the latter he uncovered the vast garden with its ornamental waterways and reconstructed the planting pattern of trees and shrubs, using the Fiorellian method to obtain plaster casts of roots.

It is sad that Spinazzola, who was dismissed from office when the Fascists came to power, published no reports on his work while he was in post, and the buildings along Via dell'Abbondanza were seriously damaged by the bombing of Pompeii carried out by the Allied air forces in September 1943. Earlier in the same year, Spinazzola himself died, and the proofs and blocks of the book that he was preparing were destroyed by bombing in Milan. Much of what he had achieved seemed destined to be lost. It was thanks only to the filial devotion of his son-in-law Salvatore Aurigemma that the book was reconstituted and published in three monumental tomes of great learning (presented in almost unreadably florid prose) in 1953.[7]

The most dynamic and long-serving director of Pompeii was Amedeo Maiuri, who succeeded Spinazzola in 1923, having gained his archaeological spurs on the Greek island of Rhodes. He stayed in charge until 1961, maintaining his position through the Fascist era, the difficult wartime years (he was himself wounded during the Allied bombing of Pompeii), and for a further 16 years of the post-war period. His best work belongs to the pre-war period, when he excavated *insulae* 7 and 10 in Region I, uncovering such finely decorated houses as the House of the Ephebe, the House of the Priest Amandus, and the House of the Menander, beside completing the excavation of the Villa of the Mysteries outside the Herculaneum Gate. Elsewhere in Pompeii he excavated the Large Palaestra (Campus) next to the amphitheatre. While all this was going on, he also found time to resume in 1927 the massive task of unearthing part of the centre of Herculaneum, a project begun under the Bourbons in 1828 but abandoned by them in 1855. These excavations were published (according to the standards of the time) with exemplary promptitude and thoroughness, both in regular reports in the standard archaeological journal *Notizie degli scavi* and in sumptuous monographs produced by the Istituto Poligrafico dello Stato – notably those on the Villa of the Mysteries (1931), the House of the Menander and its silver treasure (1933), and the architecture of the newly excavated parts of Herculaneum (1958).[8]

More importantly, Maiuri made the first systematic attempts to use excavation and the study of standing masonry to trace the historical evolution of Pompeii before 79. Among his many contributions was a stratigraphical exploration beneath the final level in the House of the Surgeon to try to determine whether the impluviate *atrium* had been preceded by an earlier phase. In the forum he sunk trenches along the east side and established that the grand Imperial-age buildings had been preceded by shops and houses. His study of the city's fortifications established a chronological sequence of phases running through from the sixth century to the time of Sulla's siege in 89 BC (though he failed to recognise, despite finding clear evidence to the contrary, that the earliest circuit of walls enclosed the same area as the later ones rather than simply defending the 'old city'). Finally, in 1942 he published his important survey of the effects of the earthquake of AD 62, using the evidence of structural repairs to build up a picture of activity during Pompeii's last phase.[9]

In the immediate aftermath of the war a first major discovery was the so-called Imperial Villa, a luxurious residence built into the walls to the south of the Marine Gate and possibly abandoned after the earthquake of 62, when the foundations for an enlargement of the temple of Venus were sunk into it. The exposure of this complex was one of the few positive outcomes of the Allied bombing, which severely damaged the overlying structures, including the site antiquarium.

Unfortunately, the last years of Maiuri's superintendency were marred by the indecent haste of his programme to clear the unexcavated areas in the south-east of the city. The work was sponsored by construction companies who provided manpower and took the spoil from the digging to use as ballast in the Naples-Salerno motorway; the resultant commercial imperatives led to a disastrous decline in recording standards and a neglect of the processes of restoration and conservation. After Maiuri's retirement in 1962, large parts of Regions I and II remained exposed, without publication and without adequate protection against the elements (75). Some houses have been published since the 1970s, but not by archaeologists who were involved in the original excavations, and in the meantime deterioration of the fabric has led to the collapse of walls and the loss of wall-paintings.

The last four decades have seen a slackening of the pace of excavation and an emphasis upon the consolidation and documentation of buildings already unearthed. With the exception of a few selected sites, notably the House of C. Julius Polybius, that of M. Fabius Rufus, and that of the Chaste Lovers, there have been no major new excavations in the city: most resources have been directed not to the area within the walls, which has scheduled-monument status and is safe from interference, but to the surrounding territory, where sites are constantly under threat from modern development. In such excavations as have been undertaken in the city, there has been a policy of careful recording, and structures have been conserved and restored as work proceeds, which means that progress is slow but that more information is retained and the buildings are better preserved for posterity.

Concern for the deterioration of Pompeii's fabric was heightened in the wake of the serious earthquake of November 1980, which caused some structures to collapse and many others to be drastically weakened. As a consequence, campaigns of photographic and computer-assisted documentation, already started in the late 1970s under the aegis of the then superintendent Fausto Zevi, became a top priority. Among the most important was the recording of the city's paintings and mosaics by the Istituto Centrale per il Catalogo e la Documentazione in Rome, which contributed directly to the publication of a monumental eleven-volume photographic encyclopaedia *Pompei, pitture e mosaici* (1990-2003). Another project, sponsored by IBM in the late 1980s, led to the creation of a database of information on all aspects of the city's archaeological legacy, accessible from computer terminals in a new museum at Boscoreale.

Along with campaigns of straightforward recording have gone projects whose purpose is to analyse and reinterpret past excavations, especially those which have never been adequately published. Many of these have involved the participation of non-Italian teams. Pride of place must go to the German 'Häuser in Pompeji' project, which examines individual houses with special emphasis on those with extensive remains of wall-paintings. Other researchers, rather than limiting themselves to single houses, have examined groups of houses or whole blocks, attempting to trace their structural history, with its complex patterns of changing property boundaries. Such projects include the work of researchers from the University of Perugia on a couple of small triangular *insulae* in Region VI and the programme directed by the present writer in the Insula of the Menander.[10]

75 Detail of a room excavated in the 1950s (I.12.16, room 2), showing painted wall plaster left exposed to the elements. Much of the plaster of the right-hand wall has collapsed. *Photograph L.A. Ling*

Other projects not yet published include those of an Anglo-Italian team in I.9 and of an Anglo-American team in VI.1.

Both of the last two projects have included excavations beneath the level of AD 79. It is now recognised that selective digging is an essential concomitant of any study of historical development. The work of M. Fulford and A. Wallace-Hadrill in the House of Amarantus has produced important new evidence on the development of Pompeii's eastern quarter.[11] It has also shown, in the wake of the pioneering studies of Pompeian gardens by Wilhelmina Jashemski,[12] perhaps the outstanding research achievement of the past half-century, the value of scientific analyses of botanical and zoological evidence. Microscopic examination of seeds, pollen and animal bones, by enabling the identification of flora and fauna, has added a whole new dimension to our understanding of life in the ancient city.

Pompeii has come a long way since the pillage of the first excavations. What of the future? There is no rush to complete the uncovering of the parts of the city which remain buried: much remains to be done in the areas already exposed, both in respect of conservation and in terms of analysis and interpretation. At the same time there is now a recognition of the need to balance the demands of the archaeologists, who wish to extract the maximum information from the site, with the obligation to present Pompeii to the general public. This, however, introduces a whole range of new problems. The erection of modern signboards, the creation of specified routes through the city, the use of weedkillers to control invasive vegetation, the closure and grassing of the forum area to prevent erosion and reduce the resultant 'dust storms' – these are some of the many unfortunate measures necessitated by the management of a vast open-air museum which attracts nearly two million visitors a year.

At the time of writing new pressures have been created by the resurgence of a problem which is far more serious: the threat of vandalism and theft. The removal of wall-paintings from a little-known house in Region I in 1977, the already mentioned stealing of statues from the garden of the Vettii in 1978, the occasional disappearance of isolated sculptures, and (more recently) the taking of a stone well-head from the House of the Ceii and of wall-paintings from the House of the Chaste Lovers – all bear witness to the dangers to which the remains are exposed. There is now a real possibility that all portable objects, and even many mosaics and wall-paintings, will have to be taken into safe stores and replaced *in situ* by facsimiles. If this happens, it will be a new tragedy for Pompeii. And in the background there is still the volcano, ominously silent since 1944. At any time it could erupt again and spew ash and clinkers over the surrounding region. If such an eruption repeated the explosive force of the one in 79, the buried city, which has been reclaimed for the modern world by successive generations of excavators, could be lost once more.

NOTES

FURTHER READING

INDEX

NOTES

The references given here, apart from the ancient texts, concentrate primarily on specialist studies, on recent discoveries and on controversies. For more general literature, including works here cited only by the author's name and date of publication, see the section 'Further Reading'. For accounts of individual buildings a full and up-to-date bibliography is available in Coarelli 2002. Abbreviations: *CIL* = *Corpus Inscriptionum Latinarum.*

CHAPTER 1

1 Pliny, *Epistulae* 6.16; 6.20; Cooley and Cooley 2004: 32-7, C9, C12
2 See Sigurdsson, Cashdollar and Sparks 1982
3 F. Haverfield, *Ancient Town-Planning* (Oxford 1913), 63-8
4 See the reports on Japanese excavations from 1993 to 1997, published in *Opuscula pompeiana* 4 (1994) 23-62; 5 (1995) 53-67; 6 (1996) 51-62; 7 (1997) 143-58; 8 (1998) 111-34
5 R. Ling, 'A stranger in town: finding the way in an ancient city', *Greece and Rome* Second series 37 (1990) 204-14
6 A. De Simone and S.C. Nappo (eds), *...Mitis Sarni opes* (Naples 2000)
7 A. Mau, *Geschichte der decorativen Wandmalerei in Pompeji* (Berlin 1882)

CHAPTER 2

1 Fundamental on the city-walls and urban development are S. De Caro, 'Nuove indagini sulle fortificazioni di Pompei', *Annali dell'Istituto Universitario Orientale [Napoli]. Sezione di Archeologia e Storia Antica* 7 (1985) 75-114; and 'Lo sviluppo urbanistico di Pompei', *Atti e memorie della Società Magna Grecia* Third series 1 (1992) 67-90
2 Fulford and Wallace-Hadrill 1999
3 F. Zevi, 'Urbanistica di Pompei', in *La regione sotterrata dal Vesuvio: studi e prospettive* (Atti del Convegno Internazionale 11-15 Novembre 1979) (Naples 1982), 353-65
4 S.C. Nappo, in Laurence and Wallace-Hadrill 1997: 96-7
5 S.C. Nappo, in Laurence and Wallace-Hadrill 1997: 93-6
6 For various theories regarding the origin of the name see A. Varone, *Pompei, i misteri di una città sepolta* (Rome 2000), 16

7   The evidence is collected in M. Cristofani, M. Pandolfini Angeletti and G. Coppola (eds), *Corpus Inscriptionum Etruscarum 2.2, Inscriptiones et in Latio et in Campania repertae* (Rome 1996), 59-64, nos 8747-75; see also Fulford and Wallace-Hadrill 1999: 82-4, 110-12

8   Strabo, *Geography* 5.4.8; Cooley and Cooley 2004: 8, A5

9   S. De Caro, *Saggi nell'area del tempio di Apollo a Pompei. Scavi stratigrafici di A. Maiuri nel 1931-32 e 1942-43* (Naples: Istituto Universitario Orientale, Dipartimento di Studi del Mondo Classico e del Mediterraneo Antico, Quaderni 3) (1986)

10   A. D'Ambrosio, *La stipe votiva in località Bottaro (Pompei)* (Naples 1984)

11   M. Bonghi Jovino (ed.), *Ricerche a Pompei. L' Insula 5 della Regio VI dalle origini al 79 d.C. I. Campagne di scavo 1976-1979* (Rome 1984); A. D'Ambrosio and S. De Caro, 'Un contributo all'architettura e all'urbanistica di Pompei in età ellenistica. I saggi nella casa VII 4, 62', *Annali dell'Istituto Universitario Orientale [Napoli]. Sezione di Archeologia e Storia Antica* 11 (1989) 173-215

12   Fulford and Wallace-Hadrill 1999

13   A. Maiuri, 'Studi e ricerche sulla fortificazione di Pompei', *Monumenti antichi* 33 (1929) 113-286; cf. De Caro, 'Nuove indagini' (above, note 1)

14   D'Ambrosio and De Caro 1989 (above, note 11)

15   H. Eschebach, *Die Stabianer Thermen in Pompeji* (Denkmäler antiker Architektur 13) (Berlin 1979)

16   A. Varone, in *Pompei. L'informatica al servizio di una città antica* (Rome 1988), 36; followed e.g. by S.C. Nappo, in *Rivista di studi pompeiani* 2 (1988) 191; 6 (1993-94) 95-8; and in Laurence and Wallace-Hadrill 1997: 120

17   A. Hoffmann, in F. Zevi (ed.), *Pompei 79. Raccolta di studi per il decimonono centenario dell'eruzione vesuviana* (Naples 1979), 111-15; idem, 'Ein Beitrag zum Wohnen in vorrömischen Pompeji,' *Architectura* 10 (1980) 1-14

18   S.C. Nappo, 'Pompei: la casa *Regio I, ins.* 20, n. 4 nelle sue fasi. Considerazioni e problemi', in L. Franchi dell'Orto (ed.), *Ercolano 1738-1988: 250 anni di ricerca archeologica. Atti del Convegno Internazionale Ravello-Ercolano-Napoli-Pompei 30 ottobre-5 novembre 1988* (Ministero per i Beni Culturali ed Ambientali, Soprintendenza Archeologica di Pompei, Monografie, 6) (Rome 1993), 667-76; 'Alcuni esempi di tipologie di case popolari della fine III, inizio II secolo a.C. a Pompei', *Rivista di studi pompeiani* 6 (1993-94) 77-104; and in Laurence and Wallace-Hadrill 1997: 99-120

19   A. Wallace-Hadrill, 'Rethinking the Roman *atrium* house', in Laurence and Wallace-Hadrill 1997: 219-40

20   For this technique, K. Peterse, *Steinfachwerk in Pompeji. Bautechnik und Architektur* (Amsterdam 1999). Generally on building techniques J.-P. Adam, *Roman Building: Materials and Techniques* (London 1994)

21   J.-A. Dickmann, 'The peristyle and the transformation of domestic space in hellenistic Pompeii', in Laurence and Wallace-Hadrill 1997: 121-36

22   Zanker 1998: 46-9

23   For recent findings suggesting that the present colonnades were erected no earlier than the first century AD see A. Carandini, in P.G. Guzzo (ed.), *Pompei. Scienza e società* (250° Anniversario degli Scavi di Pompei. Convegno Internazionale Napoli, 25-27 novembre 1998) (Milan 2001), 127-8; but Carandini's conclusions are challenged in the same volume (159-60) by F. Coarelli

24   E. Vetter, *Handbuch der italischen Dialekte* (Heidelberg 1953), 49-50, no. 11; Cooley and Cooley 2004: 9, A9

25   Vetter, *Handbuch*, 52, no. 18; Cooley and Cooley 2004: 10-11, A12

26   A. Laidlaw, *The First Style in Pompeii: Painting and Architecture* (Rome 1985); Ling 1991: 12-22

27   M. Donderer, 'Das pompejanische Alexandermosaik – ein östliches Importstuck?', in *Das antike Rom und der Osten. Festschrift für Klaus Parlasca zum 65. Geburtstag* (Erlanger Forschungen A 56) (Erlangen 1990), 19-31

CHAPTER 3

1   For the sequence of events in relation to the legal status of Pompeii, V. Weber, 'Entstehung und Rechtsstellung der römischen Gemeinde Pompeji', *Klio* 57 (1975) 179-206

2   Vetter, *Handbuch* (Chapter 2, note 24), 54-7, nos 23-8; Cooley and Cooley 2004: 19, B5

3   Castrén 1975: 85-92

4   Cicero, *Pro Sulla* 60-2; Cooley and Cooley 2004: 22-3, B15

5   *CIL* x, no. 844; Cooley and Cooley 2004: 20, B9

6   Zanker 1998: 65-8

7   *CIL* x, no. 852; Cooley and Cooley 2004: 20-1, B10

8   For a different view, which ascribes the conversion of the Capitolium to a phase of voluntary Romanisation before the Social War, see H. Lauter, in *Jahrbuch des Deutschen Archäologischen Instituts* 94 (1979) 430-4

9   *CIL* x, no. 819

10   *CIL* x, no. 829; Cooley and Cooley 2004: 21, B11

11   H. Eschebach, *Die städtebauliche Entwicklung des antiken Pompeji (Mitteilungen des Deutschen Archäologischen Instituts, Römische Abteilung* Ergänzungsheft 17) (Heidelberg 1970), 56-7

12   V.M. Strocka, *Casa del Labirinto (VI 11, 8-10)* (Häuser in Pompeji 4) (Munich 1991), 68-9

13   F. Zevi, 'La città sannitica. L'edilizia privata e la Casa del Fauno', in F. Zevi (ed.), *Pompei* I (Naples 1991), 47-74, especially 73-4; 'Pompei dalla città sannitica alla colonia sillana: per un'interpretazione dei dati archeologici', in M. Cébeillac-Gervasoni (ed.), *Les élites municipales de l'Italie péninsulaire des Gracques à Néron. Actes de la table ronde de Clermont-Ferrand (28-30 novembre 1991)* (Collection de l'École Française de Rome 215, Collection du Centre Jean Bérard 13) (Naples and Rome 1996), 125-38, especially 132-6

14   For the evidence of this union see R. Ling, *The Insula of the Menander at Pompeii* I: *The Structures* (Oxford 1997), 55, 79-81, 164-5

15   Vitruvius, *De Architectura* 6.9

16   Wallace-Hadrill 1994: 57-9

17   Vitruvius, *De Architectura* 7.5.2; cf. 5.6.9

CHAPTER 4

1   *CIL* x, no. 820; Cooley and Cooley 2000: 92-3, E32

2   *CIL* x, no. 787; Cooley and Cooley 2000: 84-5, E1

3   J.J. Dobbins, L.F. Ball, J.G. Cooper, S.L. Gavel, S. Hay, 'Excavations in the Sanctuary of Apollo at Pompeii, 1997', *American Journal of Archaeology* 102 (1998) 739-56

4   *CIL* x, no. 816; Cooley and Cooley 2000: 96-7, E39. For the spelling 'Mammia' (against the 'Mamia' used by most modern writers) Kockel, *Grabbauten* (below, note 18), 58-9

5   J.J. Dobbins, 'The altar in the sanctuary of the Genius of Augustus in the forum at Pompeii,' *Mitteilungen des Deutschen Archäologischen Instituts. Römische Abteilung* 99 (1992) 251-63

6   *CIL* x, nos 833-4; Cooley and Cooley 2004: 66-7, D51

7   For this view see C.P.J. Ohlig, *De Aquis Pompeiorum. Das Castellum Aquae in Pompeji: Herkunft, Zuleitung und Verteilung des Wassers* (Nijmegen 2001)

8   *CIL* x, no. 817; Cooley and Cooley 2004: 81, D106

9   Tiberian date: Mau 1902: 111-12. On the basis of the wall-paintings W. Ehrhardt (*Stilgeschichtliche Untersuchungen an römischen Wandmalereien von der späten Republik bis zur Zeit Neros* (Mainz 1987), 5-7, 119-20) would go even later, to the reign of Nero. Others prefer an Augustan date: e.g. L. Richardson Jr, 'Concordia and Concordia Augusta: Rome and Pompeii,' *La Parola del passato* 33 (1978) 260-72, especially 267-9; Zanker

1998: 93-101. Inscriptions: *CIL* x, nos 810-11: Cooley and Cooley 2004: 98-100, E42

10 Identification: Zanker 1998: 85-7. Dating after 62: J.J. Dobbins, 'The Imperial Cult Building in the forum at Pompeii', in A. Small (ed.), *Subject and Ruler: the Cult of the Ruling Power in Classical Antiquity (Journal of Roman Archaeology* Supplementary Series 17) (Ann Arbor 1996), 99-114. But the presence of Third Style wall-paintings in subsidiary rooms suggests an earlier date: Mau, *Geschichte* (Chapter 1, note 7), 410; J. Overbeck and A. Mau, *Pompeji in seinen Gebäuden, Alterthümern und Kunstwerken* (Leipzig 1884), 131

11 *CIL* x, no. 794; Cooley and Cooley 2004: 16, A23

12 Zanker 1998: 105-7

13 For this phenomenon (which he dates after the earthquake of AD 62) see Nappo, 'Pompei: la casa *Regio* I, *ins.* 20, n. 4' (Chapter 2, note 18)

14 J.-A. Dickmann, *Domus frequentata. Anspruchsvolles Wohnen im pompejanischen Stadthaus* (Munich 1999), 301-12

15 Dickmann (see last note), 313-22

16 P. Zanker, 'Die Villa als Vorbild des späten pompejanischen Wohngeschmacks', *Jahrbuch des Deutschen Archäologischen Instituts* 94 (1979) 460-523 (reproduced in Zanker 1998: 135-203)

17 But for the view that the existing façade of the sanctuary, together with its marble veneer, represents a post-62 rebuilding see J.J. Dobbins, 'Problems of chronology, decoration, and urban design in the forum at Pompeii,' *American Journal of Archaeology* 98 (1994) 629-94, especially 663-8

18 Pompeian cemeteries: see especially V. Kockel, *Die Grabbauten vor dem Herkulaner Tor in Pompeji* (Beiträge zur Erschliessung hellenistischer und kaiserzeitlicher Skulptur und Architektur 1) (Mainz 1983); A. D'Ambrosio and S. De Caro, *Un impegno per Pompei. Fotopiano e documentazione della necropoli di Porta Nocera* (Milan 1983)

19 For a different view on the position of the *pomerium* see F. Senatore, 'Necropoli e società nell'antica Pompei: considerazioni su un sepolcreto di poveri', in idem (ed.), *Pompei, il Vesuvio e la penisola Sorrentina* (Atti del secondo ciclo di conferenze di geologia, storia e archeologia Pompei, Istituto 'B. Longo', ottobre 1997-febbraio 1998) (Rome 1999), 91-121, especially 100-02

20 This view is argued by H. Mouritsen in a forthcoming article ('Inscriptions, burial and class. Epigraphy and social history in Pompeii, Ostia and Imperial Italy') which he has kindly let me read in advance of publication

21 Senatore, 'Necropoli e società' (above, note 19)

22 For the identification of the owner of this tomb, traditionally ascribed to A. Umbricius Scaurus, see Kockel, *Grabbauten* (above, note 18), 83-4

23 S.T.A.M. Mols and E.M. Moormann, '*Ex parvo crevit.* Proposta per una lettura iconografica della Tomba di Vestorius Priscus fuori Porta Vesuvio a Pompei', *Rivista di studi pompeiani* 6 (1993-94) 15-52

CHAPTER 5

1 Tacitus, *Annales* 14.17; Cooley and Cooley 2004: 60-1, D34

2 Tacitus, *Annales* 15.22.5; Seneca, *Quaestiones naturales* 6.1.1-3 (wrongly dating the event to AD 63); Cooley and Cooley 2004: 28-9, C1-2. On earthquake repairs, J.-P. Adam, 'Observations techniques sur les suites du séisme de 62 à Pompéi', in *Tremblements de terre, éruptions volcaniques et vie des hommes dans la Campagnie antique* (Bibliothèque de l'Institut Français de Naples, Second series, 7) (Naples: Centre Jean Bérard: 1986), 67-87. On the social and economic effects, J. Andreau, 'Histoires des séismes et histoire économique: le tremblement de terre de Pompéi (62 ap. J.C.),' *Annales économies sociétés civilisations* 28 (1973), 369-95. Restoration of temple of Isis: *CIL* x, no. 846; Cooley and

Cooley 2004: 31, C5. The extent of the reconstruction was possibly exaggerated: see N. Blanc, H. Eristov, and M. Fincker, 'A fundamento restituit? Réfections dans le temple d'Isis à Pompéi', *Revue archéologique* (2000), 227-309

3 M. Fulford and A. Wallace-Hadrill, 'The House of Amarantus at Pompeii (I, 9, 11-12): an interim report on survey and excavations in 1995-96', *Rivista di studi pompeiani* 7 (1995-96) 77-113, especially 107-08

4 Suetonius, *Nero* 20.2; Tacitus, *Annales* 15.33-34

5 Pliny, *Epistulae* 6.20.3

6 H. Mouritsen, 'Order and disorder in late Pompeian politics', in Cébeillac-Gervasoni, *Les élites municipales* (Chapter 3, note 13), 139-44

7 S.C. Nappo, 'L'impianto idrico a Pompei nel 79 d.C. Nuovi dati', in N. de Haan and G.M.C. Jansen, *Cura aquarum in Campania* (Proceedings of the Ninth International Congress on the History of Water Management and Hydraulic Engineering in the Mediterranean Region, Pompeii, 1-8 October 1994) (Leiden 1996), 37-45

8 J.J. Dobbins, 'Problems of chronology' (Chapter 4, note 17); K. Wallat, 'Der Zustand des Forums von Pompeji am Vorabend des Vesuvausbruchs 79 n.Chr', in T. Fröhlich and L. Jacobelli (eds), *Archäologie und Seismologie. La regione vesuviana dal 62 al 79 d.C. Problemi archeologici e sismologici* (Colloquium Boscoreale 26.-27. November 1993) (Munich 1995), 75-92; K. Wallat, *Die Ostseite des Forums von Pompeji* (Frankfurt 1997)

9 G. Guadagno, 'Documenti epigrafici ercolanesi relativi ad un terremoto', in Fröhlich and Jacobelli, *Archäologie und Seismologie* (see last note), 119-30

10 *CIL* x, no. 1018; Cooley and Cooley 2004: 135, F109

11 A. Varone, 'L'organizzazione del lavoro in una bottega di decoratori: le evidenze dal recente scavo pompeiano lungo Via dell'Abbondanza', *Mededelingen van het Nederlands Instituut te Rome* 54 (1995) 124-36

CHAPTER 6

1 On this question see Jongman 1988: 108-12 (with earlier bibliography); cf. A. Wallace-Hadrill, in B. Rawson (ed.), *Marriage, Divorce, and Children in Ancient Rome* (Oxford 1991), 98-103 (reproduced in Wallace-Hadrill 1994: 98-103)

2 E. De Carolis, G. Patricelli and A. Ciarallo, 'Rinvenimenti di corpi umani nell'area urbana di Pompei', *Rivista di studi pompeiani* 9 (1998) 75-123

3 M. Henneberg and R.J. Henneberg, 'Human skeletal material from Pompeii', in A. Ciarallo and E. De Carolis (eds), *Pompeii. Life in a Roman Town* (exhibition catalogue) (Milan 1999), 51-3

4 The view of J.L. Franklin (*Pompeii: the Electoral Programmata, Campaigns and Politics, A.D. 71-9* (Papers and Monographs of the American Academy in Rome 28) (Rome 1980)) that the elections – for the duovirate at least – were actually uncontested, with the number of candidates in any given year equalling the number of posts available, is based on unreliable arguments and is certainly to be rejected: see Mouritsen 1988: 37-41

5 R.I. Curtis, 'A. Umbricius Scaurus of Pompeii', in R.I. Curtis (ed.), *Studia Pompeiana et classica in Honor of Wilhelmina F. Jashemski* I: *Pompeiana* (New York 1988), 19-50

6 *CIL* x, no. 846; Cooley and Cooley 2004: 31, C5

7 On the architecture K. Ohr, *Die Basilika in Pompeji* (Denkmäler antiker Architektur 17) (Berlin and New York 1991). Graffiti: *CIL* iv, nos 1780-1952, especially 1842 and 1904: Cooley and Cooley 2004: 77, D86; 79, D103

8 Generally on the temple and on the Triangular Forum, J.A.K.E. De Waele, *Il tempio dorico del foro triangolare di Pompei* (Studi della Soprintendenza Archeologica di Pompei 2) (Rome 2002)

9 Vetter, *Handbuch* (Chapter 2, note 24), 52, no. 18; Cooley and Cooley 2004: 10-11, A12

10 S. De Caro, 'La lucerna d'oro di Pompei: un dono di Nerone a Pompei', in *I culti della*

Campania antica. Atti del Convegno Internazionale di Studi in ricordo di Nazarena Valenza Mele: Napoli, 15-17 maggio 1995 (Rome 1998), 239-44

11 For this interpretation see S. De Caro, in F. Zevi (ed.), *Pompei I* (1991), 41-2

12 Blanc, Eristov, and Fincker, 'A fundamento restituit?' (Chapter 5, note 2)

13 *CIL* x, no. 824; Cooley and Cooley 2004: 93, E34

14 Dobbins, 'Altar' (Chapter 4, note 5)

15 The suggestion that this building was a public library (L. Richardson, 'The libraries of Pompeii', *Archaeology* 30 (1977) 394-402; idem, *Pompeii. An Architectural History* (Baltimore and London 1988), 273-5) is unconvincing: see R. Ling in *Journal of Roman Archaeology* 4 (1991) 252-3. For identification and dating see Chapter 4, note 10

16 Boyce 1937; Orr 1999; T. Fröhlich, *Lararien- und Fassadenbilder in den Vesuvstädten* (*Mitteilungen des Deutschen Archäologischen Instituts, Römische Abteilung* Ergänzungsheft 32) (Mainz 1991)

17 A. Varone, *Presenze giudaiche e cristiane a Pompei* (Quaderni della Società per lo Studio e la Divulgazione dell'Archeologia Biblica 1) (Naples 1979), especially 72-8

18 Statistics of *terra sigillata* at Pompeii: G. Pucci, 'Le terre sigillate italiche, galliche, e orientali', in R. Annecchino and A. Carandini (eds), *L'instrumentum domesticum di Ercolano e Pompei nella prima età imperiale* (Rome 1977), 9-21

19 Strabo, *Geography* 5.4.8; Martial, *Epigrammata* 4.44. References to Vesuvian wine: Pliny, *Natural History* 14.22, 34-5; Columella, *Res Rustica* 3.2.10, 27. Drawbacks of Pompeian wine: Pliny, *Natural History* 14.70. Generally on Pompeian wine production and trade, A. Tchernia, 'Il vino: produzione e commercio', in F. Zevi (ed.) *Pompei 79. Raccolta di studi per il decimonono centenario dell'eruzione vesuviana* (Naples 1979), 87-96

20 Recently excavated farm: S. De Caro, *La villa rustica in località Villa Regina a Boscoreale* (Rome 1994). Vineyards in the city: Jashemski 1979 : 201-32

21 Columella, *Res Rustica* 12.10.1 (onions); Pliny, *Natural History* 19.140 (cabbages). Generally on vegetables and fruit identified at Pompeii, Jashemski and Meyer 2002; cf. Cooley and Cooley 2004: 167, H31 (labelled jars). Agricultural produce referred to in graffiti: Varone, *Pompei, i misteri* (Chapter 2, note 6), 57-62

22 Cato, *De Agricultura* 22.3-4; 135.2; Cooley and Cooley 2004: 168, H35

23 Pliny, *Natural History* 31.94 ; Cooley and Cooley 2004: 164, H18. On A. Umbricius Scaurus and his production, Curtis, *art. cit.* (above, note 5); Cooley and Cooley 2004: 165-6, H20-9

24 Moeller 1976; Jongman 1988: 155-86

25 McGinn 2002; for a more cautious view Wallace-Hadrill 1995

26 Arguments for a date late in the reign of Claudius are presented by A.M. Small, 'The shrine of the imperial family in the Macellum at Pompeii', in Small, *Subject and Ruler* (see Chapter 4, note 10), 115-36

27 Guild hall of fullers: e.g. Moeller 1976: 57-71. The slave market theory, credited to E. Fentress, is cited by E. De Albentiis in Coarelli 2002: 132-3 (cf. 398). For the dedicatory inscriptions and dating see Chapter 4, note 9

28 See Eschebach, *Stabianer Thermen* (Chapter 2, note 15)

29 P. Bargellini, 'Le Terme Centrali di Pompei', in *Les thermes romains. Actes de la table ronde organisé par l'École Française de Rome (Rome, 11-12 novembre 1988)* (Collection de l'École Française de Rome 142) (Rome 1991), 115-28

30 *CIL* ii, no. 5181

31 cf. De Waele, *Tempio dorico* (above, note 8), 328-32

32 Generally on the amphitheatre and shows at Pompeii, D.L. Bomgardner, *The Story of the Roman Amphitheatre* (London and New York 2000), 39-58; L. Jacobelli, *Gladiators at Pompeii* (Los Angeles 2003). Posters: P. Sabbatini Tumolesi, *Gladiatorum paria. Annunci di spettacoli gladiatorii a Pompei* (Rome 1980). Maius poster: *CIL* iv, no. 1179; Cooley and Cooley 2004: 53

33 Seat sponsorship: *CIL* x, nos 853-7. Cuspius Pansa inscriptions: *CIL* x, nos 858-9. Cf.

Cooley and Cooley 2004: 46-7, D1-7

34 Wallace-Hadrill 1994: 91-117

35 Plutarch, *Lucullus* 41.3-6

36 Dickmann, *Domus frequentata* (Chapter 4, note 14), 281-7

37 F. Pirson, 'Rented accommodation at Pompeii: the evidence of the *Insula Arriana Polliana* VI.6', in Laurence and Wallace-Hadrill 1997: 165-81

38 For a colour-coded plan of the distribution of different types of buildings see H. Eschebach, 'Erläuterungen zum Plan von Pompeji', in B. Andreae and H. Kyrieleis (eds), *Neue Forschungen in Pompeji* (Recklinghausen 1975), 331 f

39 Streets and traffic flow: S. Tsujimura, 'Ruts in Pompeii – the traffic system in the Roman city', *Opuscula pompeiana* 1 (1991) 58-86

40 Water supply: H. Eschebach, 'Probleme des Wasserversorgung Pompejis', *Cronache pompeiane* 5 (1979) 24-60; Ohlig, *De Aquis Pompeiorum* (Chapter 4, note 7)

41 Street fountains: H. Eschebach and T. Schäfer, 'Die öffentlichen Laufbrunnen Pompejis. Katalog und Beschreibung', *Pompeii Herculaneum Stabiae* 1 (1983) 11-40

42 Vitruvius, *De Architectura* 8.6.2; Frontinus, *De Aquis Urbis Romae* 2.118

43 A. Varone, in *Rivista di studi pompeiani* 5 (1991-92) 196

CHAPTER 7

1   For the material covered by this chapter see the titles cited in 'Further Reading', especially Cooley 2003. Ancient sources for the impact of the eruption: Cooley and Cooley 2004: 41-3, C20-30; Marcus Aurelius, *Meditations* 4.48. Relief work: Suetonius, *Titus* 8.3; Dio Cassius 66.24.1, 3-4; Cooley and Cooley 2004: 40, C17-18. Post-eruption salvage and plunder: Cooley 2003: 50-64

2   The texts of the inscriptions are lost, but see F. Bianchini, *La istoria universale provata con monumenti e figurata con simboli degli antichi* (Rome 1697), 246-8; cf. J. Macrinus, *De Vesuvio* (Naples 1693), 32-41

3   *CIL* x, nos 1443; cf. 1424, 1426-7, 1435-6

4   *CIL* x, no. 1018

5   J.W. von Goethe, *Italienische Reise* (ed. H. von Einem, Hamburg 1951), 204 (entry for 13 March 1787)

6   W. Helbig, *Wandgemälde der vom Vesuv verschütterten Städte* (Leipzig 1868)

7   V. Spinazzola, *Pompei alla luce degli scavi nuovi di Via dell'Abbondanza (anni 1910-23)* (Rome 1953)

8   A. Maiuri, *La Villa dei Misteri* (Rome 1931); *La Casa del Menandro e il suo tesoro di argenteria* (Rome 1933); *Ercolano, i nuovi scavi (1927-1958)* I (Rome 1958)

9   A. Maiuri, *L'ultima fase edilizia di Pompei* (Italia romana: Campania romana 2) (Spoleto 1942). Fortifications: Maiuri, 'Studi e ricerche' (Chapter 2, note 13). Stratigraphical explorations within the city: A. Maiuri, *Alla ricerca di Pompei preromana* (Naples 1973)

10 F. Carocci, E. De Albentiis, M. Gargiulo, and F. Pesando, *Le insulae 3 e 4 della* regio *VI di Pompei. Un'analisi storico-urbanistica* (Archaeologica perusina 5) (Rome 1990); R. Ling, *The Insula of the Menander at Pompeii* I: *The Structures* (Oxford 1997)

11 Fulford and Wallace-Hadrill 1999

12 Jashemski 1979, 1993; Jashemski and Meyer 2002

FURTHER READING

The bibliography on Pompeii is vast. The following is a selection of some of the publications available in English.

GENERAL BOOKS

Bon, S.E. and Jones, R. (eds) (1997) *Sequence and Space at Pompeii*, Oxford: Oxbow Books
Carrington, R.C. (1936) *Pompeii*, Oxford: University Press
Coarelli, F. (ed.) (2002) *Pompeii*, New York: Riverside Book Company
Cooley, A.E. and Cooley, M. (2004) *Pompeii. A Sourcebook*, London: Routledge
Descoeudres, J.-P. (1994) *Pompeii Revisited. The Life and Death of a Roman Town*, Sydney: Meditarch
Étienne, R. (1992) *Pompeii. The Day a City Died*, London: Thames and Hudson
Grant, M. (1971) *Cities of Vesuvius: Pompeii and Herculaneum*, London: Weidenfeld and Nicolson
Kraus, T. and Matt, L. von (1975) *Pompeii and Herculaneum. The Living Cities of the Dead*, New York: Harry N. Abrams
Laurence, R. (1994) *Roman Pompeii. Space and Society*, London: Routledge
Mau, A. (1899, 1902) *Pompeii, its Life and Art*, First and Second editions, translated by F.W. Kelsey, London and New York: Macmillan
Zanker, P. (1998) *Pompeii: Public and Private Life*, London and Cambridge, Mass: Harvard University Press

EXHIBITION CATALOGUES

Ciarallo, A. and De Carolis, E. (eds) (1999) *Pompeii. Life in a Roman Town* (Naples and Los Angeles), Milan: Electa
Franchi Dell'Orto, L. and Varone, A. (eds) (1990-92), *Rediscovering Pompeii* (New York, Houston, Malmö, London), Rome: 'L'Erma' di Bretschneider
Ward-Perkins, J.B. and Claridge, A. (1976) *Pompeii A.D. 79*, Bristol: Imperial Tobacco Ltd

GUIDE BOOKS

Guzzo, P.G. and D'Ambrosio, A. (2002) *Pompeii: Guide to the Site*, Naples: Electa Napoli

Maiuri, A. (1954) *Pompeii*, Seventh edition (Itineraries of the Museums, Galleries and Monuments in Italy 3), translated by V. Priestley, Rome: Istituto Poligrafico dello Stato

Nappo, S.C. (1998) *Pompeii. Guide to the Lost City*, London: Weidenfeld and Nicolson

VESUVIUS AND THE ERUPTION

De Carolis, E. and Patricelli, G. (2003) *Vesuvius A.D. 79: the Destruction of Pompeii and Herculaneum*, Los Angeles: J. Paul Getty Museum

Sigurdsson, H., Cashdollar, S. and Sparks, S.R.J. (1982) 'The eruption of Vesuvius in A.D. 79: reconstruction from historical and volcanological evidence', *American Journal of Archaeology* 86: 39-51

BEGINNINGS AND EARLY HISTORY

Berry, J. (ed.) (1998) *Unpeeling Pompeii. Studies in Region I of Pompeii*, Milan: Electa

Fulford, M. and Wallace-Hadrill, A. (1999) 'Towards a history of pre-Roman Pompeii: excavations beneath the House of Amarantus (I.9.11-12), 1995-8', *Papers of the British School at Rome* 67: 37-144

PUBLIC LIFE AND POLITICS

Castrén, P. (1975) *Ordo Populusque Pompeianus. Polity and Society in Roman Pompeii* (Acta Instituti Romani Finlandiae 8), Rome

Franklin, J.L. (2001) *Pompeis difficile est. Studies in the Political Life of Imperial Pompeii*, Ann Arbor: University of Michigan Press

Mouritsen, H. (1988) *Elections, Magistrates and Municipal Élite. Studies in Pompeian Epigraphy* (*Analecta Romana Instituti Danici* Suppl. 15), Rome: 'L'Erma' di Bretschneider

DOMESTIC RELIGION

Boyce, G.K. (1937) *Corpus of the Lararia of Pompeii* (*Memoirs of the American Academy in Rome* 14), Rome

Orr, D.G. (1999) *Roman Domestic Religion. A Study of the Roman Household Deities and their Shrines at Pompeii and Herculaneum*, Ann Arbor, Michigan: UMI

ECONOMY AND PRODUCTION

Carrington, R.C. (1931) 'Studies in the Campanian *villae rusticae*', *Journal of Roman Studies* 21: 110-30

Day, J. (1931) 'Agriculture in the life of Pompeii', *Yale Classical Studies* 3: 165-208

Jongman, W. (1988) *The Economy and Society of Pompeii* (Dutch Monographs on Ancient History and Archaeology 4), Amsterdam

Mayeske, B.J.B. (2003) *Bakeries, Bakers and Bread at Pompeii: a Study in Social and Economic History*, Ann Arbor, Michigan: UMI

Moeller, W.O. (1976) *The Wool Trade of Ancient Pompeii* (Studies of the Dutch Archaeological and Historical Society 3), Leiden: Brill

Packer, J.E. (1978) 'Inns at Pompeii: a short survey', *Cronache pompeiane* 4: 5-53

PROSTITUTION

McGinn, T.A.J. (2002) 'Pompeian brothels and social history', in Stein, C. and Humphrey, J.H. (eds), *Pompeian Brothels, Pompeii's Ancient History, Mirrors and Mysteries, Art and Nature at Oplontis, and the Herculaneum Basilica (Journal of Roman Archaeology* Supplementary Series 47), Portsmouth, Rhode Island: 7-46

Wallace-Hadrill, A. (1995) 'Public honour and private shame: the urban texture of Pompeii', in Cornell, T.J. and Lomas, K. (eds), *Urban Society in Roman Italy,* London: University College, 39-62

HOUSES

Laurence, R. and Wallace-Hadrill, A. (eds) (1997) *Domestic Space in the Roman World: Pompeii and Beyond (Journal of Roman Archaeology* Supplementary Series 22), Portsmouth, Rhode Island

Wallace-Hadrill, A. (1994) *Houses and Society in Pompeii and Herculaneum,* Princeton: University Press

GARDENS

Ciarallo, A. (2001) *Gardens of Pompeii,* Rome: 'L'Erma' di Bretschneider

Jashemski, W.F. (1979, 1993) *The Gardens of Pompeii, Herculaneum and the Villas Destroyed by Vesuvius,* 2 vols, New York: Caratzas Brothers

Jashemski, W.F. and Meyer, F.G. (eds) (2002) *The Natural History of Pompeii,* Cambridge: University Press

INTERIOR DECORATION

Ling, R. (1991) *Roman Painting,* Cambridge: University Press

THE REDISCOVERY AND EXCAVATION OF POMPEII AND HERCULANEUM

Cooley, A.E. (2003) *Pompeii,* London: Duckworth

Corti, E.C. (1951) *The Destruction and Resurrection of Pompeii and Herculaneum,* London: Routledge and Kegan Paul

Leppmann, W. (1966) *Pompeii in Fact and Fiction,* London: Elek

Parslow, C.C. (1995) *Rediscovering Antiquity. Karl Weber and the Excavation of Herculaneum, Pompeii, and Stabiae,* Cambridge: University Press

Trevelyan, R. (1976) *The Shadow of Vesuvius,* London: The Folio Society

INDEX

If you are interested in purchasing other books published by Tempus,
or in case you have difficulty finding any Tempus books in your local bookshop,
you can also place orders directly through our website

www.tempus-publishing.com